Catholic Treasures
New and Old

Joanne Turpin

Catholic Treasures New and Old

Traditions, Customs and Practices

ST.
ANTHONY
MESSENGER
PRESS

CINCINNATI, OHIO

Nihil Obstat: Rev. Arthur Espelage, O.F.M.
Rev. Robert L. Hagedorn

Imprimi Potest: Rev. John Bok, O.F.M.
Provincial

Imprimatur: +Rev. Carl Moeddel, V.G.
Archdiocese of Cincinnati
November 11, 1993

The *nihil obstat* and *imprimatur* are a declaration that a book is considered to be free from doctrinal or moral error. It is not implied that those who have granted the *nihil obstat* and *imprimatur* agree with the contents, opinions or statements expressed.

Cover and book design by Julie Lonneman

ISBN 0-86716-164-7

Published by St. Anthony Messenger Press
Printed in the U.S.A.

Contents

In cherished memory of my parents

John Breuer

and

Frida Schirmer Breuer

Introduction

During a visit to Baghdad in 1979, I rejoiced at the discovery of a Catholic church just a few blocks from my hotel. Upon stepping into the church courtyard, I was at once spiritually at home, for a grotto with a statue of the Blessed Mother occupied a portion of the yard. The building itself was new, but the liturgy was as ancient as the language in which Mass was celebrated: Syriac, a dialect of the Aramaic spoken by Jesus. During Mass, while toddlers played with their mothers' rosary beads, the mothers smiled at me in welcome. Though obviously a stranger to their country, I shared their faith. In a religious sense, we were family.

Longtime Catholics steeped in their religion know in their bones the things that make up the heart and soul of Roman Catholicism. Some of these Catholic things are as essential as the Mass. Others, such as white dresses and veils for first Communion, though not essential, can have an equally strong hold on the religious imagination. At times it can be difficult to distinguish between the essentials and the trimmings, the tradition and the customs. Newcomers to Catholicism especially can be confused by the blend of traditions, customs and practices that they encounter.

The core truth of the Catholic faith is that Jesus Christ lived, died and rose from the dead that we might have life. This apostolic teaching that has come down to us through Scripture and Tradition is an unchanging reality that grounds our lives as Catholic Christians. This book will deal little with this level of Tradition.

Over two thousand years, the Church has developed other traditions such as the rituals for Mass and the sacraments, the institutional organization of church structures, the constant moral teachings that have guided people through changing situations and circumstances, the theological understanding of the revealed truths. These latter traditions can change over time, as in our own century we have seen a great many changes, for example, in the way the Mass is celebrated.

Some of these changes were made as a result of the Second Vatican Council, held in the 1960's. The world's Roman Catholic bishops gathered to address the challenges of the modern world and to renew the internal life of the Church, deliberating on issues such as liturgical reform, a more participatory role for the laity, the mission of the Church in contemporary society and ecumenism—seeking a more harmonious relationship with other faiths. In the following chapters we will look at some of these changes that took place in the church's various traditions, particularly in the last three decades.

In addition to the apostolic Tradition and the various traditions of the Church, customs and practices have grown up in a particular time and place and are linked with tradition in many people's minds, even though they do not have any weight of the official Church behind them. In the same way that families all have different ways of celebrating Thanksgiving or Christmas, the family of Catholicism has created a variety of customs around the core events and beliefs of the faith. People hold to these customs and practices with great loyalty and at times even argue vehemently with those who do things differently. We will do our best to explain some of these customs and practices, how they developed and where they belong in the life of the Church today.

Traditions, customs and practices are the threads that tie together succeeding generations of believers. During times of transition these threads may become tangled. One generation may hold firmly to practices that are almost unintelligible to a later generation, which holds just as firmly to new ideas and experiments that have developed in recent years. In the aftermath of Vatican II, some people were horrified and others exhilarated by the changes that took place.

Take the case of one parish where the parish council in a stormy session debated the pastor's proposal to remove the communion rail bordering the sanctuary. His intention was to provide easier access to the altar for liturgical ministers. All but one of the council members belonged to an older generation that had sacrificed to build the church in the 1950's. It was their religious home, with all the emotions that "home" entails.

Finally, when a break came in the heated exchange, the only young member of the group asked curiously, "What's the rail for?" The question prompted first astonishment, then explanation. These parishioners had knelt at the rail countless times for reception of the Eucharist in the past. Now, even though the rail no longer served a practical purpose, it was part of parish history, and in that sense still held meaning. For newcomers, who had never knelt at the rail and may never have knelt to receive Communion, surely it seemed an obsolete piece of architecture. An understanding of the historical and emotional background was essential to resolve the question.

This story had a happy ending. Respecting the feelings of the older parishioners, the pastor offered to remove the rail in sections and use them to enclose several side altars in the church. The sacred association could be retained.

Catholics have much to treasure in their faith. Young Catholics and those received into the Church since Vatican II can discover here the many traditions and customs that others may refer to casually as "the way Catholics do things." Older Catholics may discover new ways of expressing their faith as well as reasons underlying traditions they've taken for granted.

CHAPTER ONE

The House of the Church: Sacred Space

The design and furnishings of a church teach us a great deal about the way people express their faith. In the Middle Ages, particularly in Europe, the people expressed their image of the transcendent God in magnificent churches and cathedrals. The great Romanesque and Gothic architectural styles witness to this period in the Church's history.

In our own time, our worship may take place in a scaled-down version of these soaring domes or spires. Often, when groups of Catholic immigrants came to this country, particularly from Europe, their first priority was to build a parish church, often at great personal sacrifice. They brought with them images of the great buildings in their home countries.

With the reforms in the liturgy that followed Vatican II, the architecture of church buildings changed to reflect the insights of the Council fathers. New churches were built that looked much different than the great buildings of the past. And even in the older buildings, the furnishings were rearranged to reflect the new outlook.

Let's look at a typical parish church to see the essential elements included in the worship space. Imagine that this church was built in the years before Vatican II, but has since been adapted to newer trends in church architecture recommended by the U.S. bishops in response to the reforms of the Council.

A Church Visit

Pushing open the doors we step into the vestibule, or entryway—the space that serves to make the transition from the secular world to the sacred. The vestibule is often the place where people greet each other before and after services. There might be a bulletin board here that lists parish activities and a rack to hold religious literature of interest to the congregation. After a Sunday Mass, raffle tickets, bake sales or other fund-raising activities may be conducted here.

Some churches have a soundproof room off the vestibule, with a large window facing into the church and speakers for hearing what is said in the main room of the church. This "crying room," as it is often called, gives parents a place to bring fussy babies or toddlers and still see and hear what is going on during the Mass.

From the vestibule, we enter the church proper through another set of doors. Once a church is built, the local bishop presides at a dedication ceremony, which includes incensing and anointing the altar and walls with chrism (holy oils).

Just inside the doorway is a holy water font. Catholics dip their right hands into the basin of water and bless themselves with the Sign of the Cross. Tracing the cross on ourselves with holy water says we belong to Christ and recalls our baptismal vows and spiritual cleansing.

Catholics have customarily genuflected—the right knee bent to touch the floor—before entering a pew. When the tabernacle containing the Blessed Sacrament resides in the sanctuary, genuflection is the proper mark of adoration. If the tabernacle is housed in a separate eucharistic chapel, a reverent bow from the waist is an appropriate sign of respect for the altar, which symbolizes Christ, whenever you enter or leave the church.

The main body of the church is the place where the people assemble to celebrate the liturgy. The greater part of any church is taken up by space for congregational seating, an area also referred to as the nave. Most churches have pews for seating, although newer or renovated churches may have chairs rather than pews. The seating may be arranged so that we can better see the people with whom we are worshipping.

Pews were a relatively late addition to church furnishings, an innovation resulting from the sixteenth-century Protestant Reformation, which placed the emphasis in worship on listening to readings from Scripture and lengthy sermons. Prior to this, the congregations generally stood or knelt during the service.

The choir area may be near the front of the assembly area or in a choir loft at the back of the church. The role of the choir is to lead the assembly in the music for the liturgy. The choir space may have an organ or a piano or both. Other more portable instruments may be brought in as well.

At the front of the church is the sanctuary. The altar, often slightly raised to give the assembly a better view, is the focal point of the sanctuary. The word *altar* itself comes from *altus*, or "high place." The altar symbolizes Christ. Some altars have a special "altar stone" set into the center, which contains the relics of a saint. This grew out of the practice in early Christianity of offering Mass at the tombs of martyrs. Some altars also have five crosses carved into the surface in remembrance of the five wounds of Christ at his crucifixion. Both the altar stone and the five crosses are now optional.

Many churches still have a high altar set against the back wall of the sanctuary. This is the altar where the priest said Mass in the pre-Vatican II rite. The tabernacle may be set on this back altar.

The ambo, or pulpit, from which the Word of God is proclaimed and preached shares the sanctuary with the altar. The ambo is central to the Liturgy of the Word in the same way that the altar is central to the Liturgy of the Eucharist. A simple lectern for announcements or directions from the music minister can be placed elsewhere in the sanctuary or near the space for the choir.

A chair for the priest who presides at the liturgy is also set in the sanctuary. Chairs for the other liturgical ministers— servers, readers, eucharistic ministers—may also be located here. Off to the side of the sanctuary the credence table holds the chalice and cruets, basin and finger towel and extra Communion cups and plates.

Catholics have long been accustomed to a crucifix—a cross bearing the image of Christ—hanging high above the altar on the back wall of the sanctuary. A crucifix is not mandated, however. In fact, a cross—the unadorned shape—used during the entrance procession of the Mass, then placed in a standard near the altar, may now suffice.

Candles, originally used to provide light for early morning services, came to signify Christ as the light of the world. Mounted in candlesticks, candles are placed on or near the altar and lighted for Mass and other liturgical services.

The Paschal (Easter) Candle, with its own special candlestand, occupies a prominent place in the sanctuary during the Easter Season, when it is lighted for Sunday Mass and other celebrations.The large candle is often richly ornamented with highly symbolic designs, including five grains of incense representing the wounds of the Savior and arranged in the shape of a cross, and the Greek letters Alpha and Omega, meaning Christ as the beginning and end of all things.

The Paschal Candle is also lit at other times of the year for special occasions such as baptisms and funerals. Outside of the festive Easter Season, it is kept near the baptistery, which contains the font for baptisms and perhaps also the oils used in the sacrament. This can be located either near the vestibule or near the sanctuary.

In some churches, the tabernacle resides in a eucharistic chapel separate from the main worship space. A separate chapel offers a quiet place for personal prayer outside of Mass. The cabinet-shaped tabernacle, always of precious material, holds Communion hosts to be taken to the sick. A sanctuary lamp—an oil lamp or candleholder of red glass—burns continuously near the tabernacle to indicate the Lord's presence in the form of the eucharistic bread. The tabernacle is kept locked.

Churches generally have a special place for celebrating the Sacrament of Reconciliation. In the past, every Catholic was familiar with the confessional box, a booth-like structure, with doors to provide privacy, positioned along the side wall of the church. Confessionals typically have three compartments: the priest's in the center and the penitents' on either side. Dividing screens, or grilles, within provide anonymity.

Since the rite for administering this sacrament was revised, churches have been encouraged to set aside a room where the penitent may choose either to sit face-to-face with the confessor (priest) or behind a screen that provides anonymity. People also still have the option of using the confessional.

In various parts of many churches, statues of saints are placed on pedestals or small "altars." Before each statue is a stand filled with votive candles and a kneeler for those who want to light a candle before saying a prayer. The lighted candle symbolizes an offering of prayer. The flame, like the prayer, continues after the person has left the church.

In most Catholic churches, Stations of the Cross hang on side walls, seven stations to the left and seven to the right. We will discuss this devotion in a later chapter. Though the stations need only be marked by a small wooden cross, they often show scenes depicting Jesus' journey to the cross and his death. While stations are not mandatory, the tradition is so strong that it would be rare to find a Catholic church without them.

Sacred art is intended to inspire reverence. Although styles come and go in sacred as well as secular art, stained glass never seems to lose its appeal. The light shining through the jewel-like colored glass evokes a religious mood. In a more distant time, when the majority of people were illiterate, biblical stories told through images in stained glass served as a form of religious education.

The Sacristy

The sacristy is the room where vestments, sacred vessels, linens and other liturgical objects are kept. In most churches, the sacristy is located to the side of the sanctuary. Those participating in the service may put on their vestments here. In the past the priest and altar servers emerged through the doors of the sacristy into the sanctuary to celebrate Mass, then exited the same way. Today, at least for Sunday liturgies, the entrance procession moves from the vestibule, through the congregational area, to the altar. For that reason, some churches provide a separate vesting area just off the vestibule.

Every sacristy should have a *sacrarium*, that is, a basin or sink with a drain that leads directly to the earth. The sacrarium is used to dispose of materials used for sacred purposes, for example, blessed water or blessed ashes.

Certain clothing has become associated with religious services. The most widely worn vestment is the *alb*, a full-length, wide-sleeved garment of white linen, derived from the Roman tunic. To contain its fullness, the alb may be tied at the waist with a *cincture*—a long cord with tassels at each end. Priests and bishops wear albs for liturgical ministry. Lay ministers may also wear an alb.

The *surplice*, also loose-fitting and wide-sleeved, made of white linen or cotton, is worn by a priest over a *cassock*, a long black garment. This was also the vestment worn by acolytes or altar servers. Servers today more often wear a variation of an alb.

The *stole*, a long narrow band of material worn around the neck and hanging loose in front, is the symbol of priestly ministry. A deacon also wears a stole in the manner of a sash over the left shoulder, drawn across the chest and fastened at the right side. A stole must always be worn as part of vesture by the priest celebrating Mass or administering the sacraments. It may be worn over or under the chasuble.

The *chasuble*, a full, semicircular cloak with an opening in the center for the head, is the outer garment worn by a priest for Mass. It is sleeveless, but full enough that the fabric drapes over the arms. At one time the chasuble had to be made of silk; now other materials of fine quality are also permitted.

The outer vestment for deacons is called a *dalmatic*. Cut more squarely than a chasuble, it has short sleeves and is open on the sides. Some deacons prefer wearing just alb and stole for most occasions, reserving the dalmatic for weddings and other more formal rites.

An *amice*, a piece of white linen cloth covering the shoulders and tying around the chest, may be worn under the alb. Required before Vatican II, this is now optional.

Special vestments are worn for rites such as Benediction,

which we will cover in later chapters.

The most important vessels used at Mass hold the consecrated bread and wine. They must be made of the finest materials. In the past gold was the most frequent choice, although silver-lined with gold plating was also an option. Today other materials such as stonework and ceramic may also be used. They must be finely made, durable and dignified.

The *chalice* holds the consecrated wine. The *plate* or *paten* holds the eucharistic bread on the altar. The *ciborium*, shaped much like a covered chalice, is the receptacle in which hosts are reserved in the tabernacle. The ciborium may be used in distributing consecrated hosts at Communion, although ideally the hosts used for Communion should be consecrated during the Mass at which they are used.

The *cruets*, flasks usually made of glass or crystal and covered with a stopper, are used for pouring water and wine. For large groups, a larger decanter is used for the wine.

Other vessels used at Mass or other liturgical functions include the following:

A *sprinkler*, or *aspergillum*, is a metal, bulblike container which is perforated and used for sprinkling holy water on persons or objects. A bundle of branches or an evergreen branch may also be used.

A *censer* is used for incensing persons or objects. The metal censer, once called a thurible, is generally in the form of a cup or bowl with a perforated cover, suspended on a chain or chains. Incense burned on lighted charcoal inside the censer provides the fragrant smoke that billows out as the censer is swung back and forth. A small covered dish, often called an incense boat because of its elongated shape, holds extra incense and a small spoon. Incense may also be burned in a bowl set on a stand near the altar or ambo.

At least one *altar cloth*, usually of white linen, covers the altar table. A small, square cloth, the *corporal*, is spread on the altar cloth for Mass. Sacred vessels containing the eucharistic bread and wine must be set on the corporal. At one time, the corporal was kept in a square cloth "envelope" called a *burse* when not in use.

Other linens include a *purificator*, a small linen cloth used to wipe the rim of the chalice. A purificator is also used to dry the chalice after it has been cleansed at the end of Mass.

A square-cut *chalice veil* may be draped over the chalice while it is on the credence table. This was required before Vatican II but is now optional. The silk veil may be white or match the color of the priest's vestments for Mass.

The *pall*, a square of stiffened linen was set atop the chalice before the consecration. The origin of the pall may have been a practical one: keeping insects or dust from falling into the cup. It still may be used for this purpose today.

The books with the official texts for liturgical services should always be large (for visibility) and attractively bound, in keeping with the sacredness of public worship.

The Roman Missal, the book that contains the official rite for Mass, is divided into the *Sacramentary* and the *Lectionary*. The Sacramentary contains the prayers and rubrics (that is, the rules or directives) for the celebrant. The word *rubric* is derived from the Latin for "red." These directions are printed in red while the text is set in black.

The *Lectionary* contains the assigned Scripture readings for Sundays, feasts, weekdays and special Masses. There may also be a separate Book of Gospels. The Lectionary or the Book of the Gospels may be carried in procession to show special reverence for the word of God.

For Further Reading

Gent, Barbara, and Betty Sturges. *The Altar Guild Book.* Harrisburg, Pa.: Morehouse Publishing, 1982.

Simon, Thomas G., and James M. Fitzpatrick. *The Ministry of Liturgical Environment.* Collegeville, Minn.: The Liturgical Press, 1984.

U.S. Bishops. *Environment and Art in Catholic Worship.* Washington, D.C.: The United States Catholic Conference, 1978.

CHAPTER TWO

The Mass: Sacred Action

The term *Mass* comes from Latin words of dismissal at the end of the service: *"Ite, missa est"* ("Go, you are dismissed"). This prayer is also referred to as the "Eucharistic celebration" (derived from the Greek word for "thanksgiving") or "Holy Sacrifice of the Mass." Since Vatican II, *eucharistic liturgy* has become the most appropriate term. In fact, the council's document is entitled *Constitution on the Sacred Liturgy*. *Liturgy* means "work of the people." We add "eucharistic" when we're talking about the Mass, because the official liturgy of the Church also includes the sacramental rites and the Liturgy of the Hours—both of which will be covered in later chapters.

The heart of Catholic worship since the time of the apostles has been the Sunday celebration of the Eucharist. In essence, the ritual is a memorial of the first eucharistic celebration—the sacrificial banquet of the Last Supper. Jesus and his disciples gathered around a table for the singing of psalms, blessing and breaking of bread, blessing of the cup (wine) and Jesus' offering of himself to atone for the sins of all the human race.

Because he had instructed his disciples to "do this in memory of me" (Luke 22:19), the infant Church continued to reenact the Lord's Supper. Gradually, more prayers were added and Scripture readings expanded to include the Gospels, once they were put into written form. Evidence of this basic structure of the Mass is given in the writings of St. Justin Martyr, a Palestinian-born apologist (defender of the faith) around the year 150. As he described it, all of the faithful took an active part, with one person designated to preside.

Over the ensuing centuries, historical circumstances and theological understanding resulted in the actions of the priest-celebrant in the sanctuary becoming distanced from the congregation. As the ritual grew increasingly elaborate, the faithful became silent spectators at a sacred drama. They often resorted to private devotions such as the rosary during Mass. Even today, you may still see people praying the rosary during Mass. Translation of missals—Mass prayer books—from Latin into the local language had been long forbidden. Only in the twentieth century were missals with English translation available in the United States.

From Sacred Drama to Sacred Action

As far back as the nineteenth century, a movement to reform and revitalize the liturgy got under way, with a leading role played by French and German monks. In the decades preceding Vatican II, the Benedictine Abbey of St. John in Collegeville, Minnesota, became the American center of the movement. Tentative steps toward renewal had been taken in the 1950's by Pope Pius XII.

After Vatican II, high priority was given to participation of the faithful in the sacred action of the Mass. To encourage participation, world bishops at the council voted 1,922 to 11 to allow Mass to be said in the vernacular.

Abandoning Latin, ironically, was done for the same reason that Latin was originally adopted: to make the Mass intelligible, and thus invite full involvement. The Aramaic that Jesus and his followers spoke was replaced by Greek, for that was the language generally understood in all parts of the Roman Empire where Christianity had spread. In the third century, the bishop of Rome (Pope Callistus) abandoned Greek and adopted Latin, by then the common tongue of his flock. Roman usage eventually was applied to the wider Church. Latin in time ceased to be a living language, though it continued in use not only for the Mass, but also as the official medium of communication for educated clerics.

Latin is still the official language for the Mass, and you will occasionally find parishes that schedule a Mass with prayers in Latin, but with the form of the liturgical action equivalent to the present English version.

Though responses were once primarily the province of altar servers, now all the assembly is expected to take a vocal part. We all celebrate the liturgy together. The assembly has an active and necessary role. Our responses are meant to be thoughtful affirmations of our identity as the people of God. Our "Amens" are a sign of our commitment, our affirmation of the prayer just spoken by the presider. An Alleluia is a joyous cry of "Praise the Lord."

In broadest outline, the Mass consists of four parts: Introductory Rites, Liturgy of the Word, Liturgy of the Eucharist and Concluding Rite. Not every Mass is rigidly the same, however. Options are allowed for some prayers, and leeway granted for additional ceremonies such as incensing or a sprinkling rite, or even for liturgical expressions of a cultural heritage. But the essential elements will always be present.

Vatican II placed renewed emphasis on the importance of Scripture. In the view of the council, the two major parts of the Mass, "the liturgy of the word and the liturgy of the eucharist, are so closely connected with each other that they form but one single act of worship" (*Constitution on the Sacred Liturgy*, #56). Moreover, Christ "is present in his word since it is he himself who speaks when the holy Scriptures are read in the Church" (*Liturgy*, #7).

As the Liturgy of the Word begins, the two Scripture readings preceding the Gospel are done by lay readers, or lectors, a ministerial role open to the laity since Vatican II. The best way to hear the readings is by listening attentively rather than reading along with the lector. When the readings were proclaimed in Latin, people had no choice but to follow along in their missals. Today lectors are trained in proclaiming the word of God to be heard and understood by the assembly.

In the Gospel, Jesus' words and actions come to life in our midst. For the first two readings and psalm, the assembly is seated, a position long associated with a receptivity to sacred words. As we approach the summit of the Liturgy of the Word, the reading of the Gospel, we stand as a mark of special honor. Before the Gospel is proclaimed, our acclamation, an "Alleluia," heralds the Good News. During Lent, one of four

15

other acclamations (for example, "Praise to you, Lord Jesus Christ, king of endless glory") replaces the joyful Alleluia.

Further honor may be accorded the Gospel by the celebrant's carrying the Book of Gospels aloft with solemnity to the center of the sanctuary before returning to the ambo. The book may also be incensed. Lighted candles placed by the ambo call our attention to the prominence of this part of the liturgy.

As the celebrant begins: "A reading from the holy gospel according to..." (whichever evangelist is being read that Sunday), we sign ourselves with three small Signs of the Cross: using the right thumb to trace a cross on forehead, lips and heart. This is accompanied by our praying in silent union with the celebrant that the words we are about to hear may always be in our minds, on our lips and in our hearts. The priest or deacon always reads the Gospel at Mass.

After reading the Gospel, the celebrant reverently kisses the book, and the congregation again sits to listen to the homily. A homily, commonly described as "breaking open the Word of God," takes as its starting point the Gospel and other readings of the day. The Word is made relevant to the present situation of the assembled listeners. The homily is reserved to the ordained—priest or deacon. Ordinarily, the presiding priest will give the homily.

You may hear people refer to the priest's "sermon." In the past, this was the most common term used for a religious speech. A sermon is a teaching tool and may be on any topic, not necessarily on the Scriptures. One of the reforms of Vatican II was to encourage greater attention to Scripture. Thus the sermon gave way to the homily, an exposition of Scripture.

The Liturgy of the Word concludes with a recitation of the Profession of Faith (the Nicene Creed, formulated in the fourth century) and the General Intercessions. The General Intercessions—also called Prayer of the Faithful—are the public prayer of the people in exercising their priestly function. Petitions are offered for the Church and the world, for public authorities, for those oppressed for any reason, for those who have died and for the local community and parish.

Liturgy of the Eucharist

Having been nourished by the Word of God, we prepare to be nourished by the Eucharist. This part of the ritual begins with the Preparation of the Gifts, during which the altar table is readied and the unconsecrated bread and wine are brought up by representatives of the congregation. In the early Church, people brought bread and wine from home for the liturgy, and our action today represents that custom. The collection of monetary gifts is brought forward as a sign of the community's thanksgiving for God's gifts.

The former Roman Rite (the manner in which the liturgy is to be celebrated, as authorized by the Diocese of Rome) permitted just one standard Eucharistic Prayer, called the Canon. Since the council, the liturgy has been enriched by a choice of four regular Eucharistic Prayers plus two for Masses of Reconciliation and three for use in children's liturgies.

The prayer formulas follow the same basic pattern, from Preface to the concluding Doxology, and the words of institution—the consecration—are identical in each of them. Eucharistic Prayer I (the pre-Vatican II Canon, also called the Roman Canon) enjoys the tradition of being the longest in continual use. The second prayer, modeled after an ancient formula going back to Hippolytus in the third century, has a simplicity and brevity that make it particularly appropriate for a weekday Mass. The third prayer has its roots in the Byzantine rite. The Holy Spirit is named more often than in the other prayers. The fourth prayer with its proper preface gives an account of salvation history.

The whole Eucharistic Prayer constitutes "the center and summit of the entire celebration." Through this prayer, "the entire congregation joins itself to Christ in acknowledging the great things God has done and in offering the sacrifice" (*General Instruction on the Roman Missal*, #54).

The unity of the congregation is especially underscored during the Communion rite. First, as children of God, we recite or sing together the Lord's Prayer. It is the custom in some parishes for people to join hands at this time.

The ritual sign of peace was an ancient tradition that

gradually fell into disuse. It was revived in the liturgical renewal that followed Vatican II. Some mistakenly think that this is a greeting. It actually stands for both unity and the reconciliation necessary for the community to become the one Body of Christ. The ritual comes just before Communion, recalling Jesus' words on the need to reconcile with our brothers and sisters before we approach the altar. (See Matthew 5:23-24.) The manner in which the sign is given is left up to local custom. The most common practice is a handshake along with the words, "Peace be with you."

Most Catholics these days receive the host in the hand, although it is also acceptable to have the host placed on the tongue. This latter was the practice for hundreds of years, when the host was considered too sacred for anyone to touch except for priests, whose hands are consecrated at ordination.

We believe that Jesus is fully present in either the consecrated bread or wine. For various reasons, not everyone wishes to partake of the consecrated wine. Although the communicant may not dip the host into the wine as a substitute for drinking from the cup, the minister may dip the consecrated bread into the wine and place it on the communicant's tongue. This is not customary in the United States.

Our participatory role does not end with the closing of the liturgy. Strengthened by the Word of God and nourished by the Eucharist, we are expected to proclaim that word and become the Body of Christ in the world. When the banquet is over, we are each dispatched to do something in our daily life to build the Kingdom of God on earth.

For Further Reading

Huck, Gabe. *Liturgy with Style and Grace*. Chicago: Liturgy Training Publications, 1984.

Lang, Rev. Jovian P., O.F.M. *Dictionary of the Liturgy*. New York: Catholic Book Publishing Company, 1989.

Simcoe, Mary Ann, ed. *The Liturgy Documents: A Parish Resource*. Chicago: Liturgy Training Publications, 1985.

CHAPTER THREE

The Church Year: Sacred Time

The Church year or liturgical year offers us the gift of sacred time. As the people of God, we journey through the seasons, Sundays and feasts that commemorate the story of the life of Christ and our life as the Body of Christ. The liturgical calendar marks the times of the Church at prayer.

The Church year begins on the First Sunday of Advent, in late November or early December, rather than on New Year's Day. Following the season of Advent, we celebrate the Christmas Season, and then a period of Ordinary Time, so-called because we celebrate no major feasts in this time but simply count the Sundays and weeks of the year. Lent begins on Ash Wednesday and lasts until noon on Holy Thursday. With the Mass of the Lord's Supper on Holy Thursday, we begin the Sacred Triduum, the most sacred three days in the Church year. The Easter Season extends for fifty days, from Easter Sunday until Pentecost. The remainder of the Church year counts the remaining weeks of Ordinary Time, through the seasons of summer and autumn. The final week of the Church Year begins with the Solemnity of Christ the King—reminding us that Christ is forever our goal as we journey through the year and through life.

At various times during the year, we celebrate feast days in honor of the Lord, Mary, the angels and saints. Certain days are also designated for fasting and abstinence. In addition, there are observances particular to local faith communities. Examples of these might be the anniversary of a parish church's dedication, or of a religious order's founding.

The Sunday Celebration

Because the Resurrection occurred on the first day of the week, Sunday has been considered special since the time of the apostles. We often refer to Sunday as the Lord's Day. The Gospels record that the early post-Resurrection appearances in which the Lord shared a meal with his disciples occurred on Sunday. The first Pentecost, when the Holy Spirit descended on the disciples, was also a Sunday. Not surprisingly then, Christians have always revered this day by gathering to worship.

Easter, the principal celebration of the entire year, is sometimes referred to as the "great Sunday," with Sundays in turn being called "little Easters." Each Sunday we commemorate the Paschal Mystery, the central truth of our faith: that by Jesus' death and resurrection, he overcame sin and redeemed humankind.

Advent

A period of preparation precedes the two major seasons in the year—Christmas and Easter. In the weeks of December, we observe Advent (derived from the Latin word meaning "to come"), a time of looking forward in joyful expectation to the coming of Christ into our world. This anticipation has three levels: We recall the first coming of Christ as a baby at Bethlehem; we celebrate his presence in our world today; we look to his coming at the end of time.

The Gospel that we hear on the First Sunday of Advent focuses on the end time. Jesus urges his followers to be vigilant, because no one knows the day or the hour of the final judgment. On the next two Sundays, John the Baptist calls us to repentance and conversion in order to prepare ourselves for the coming of the Lord. Advent readings from the prophets, especially Isaiah, fill us with longing and hope for the promised savior. And on the Fourth Sunday, we reflect on Mary's role in the Incarnation. Her generosity of spirit inspires us to act with generosity too. If we celebrate Advent well, we arrive at

Christmas ready to celebrate the fullness of hope it brings.

Christmas Season

Our Christmas Season customarily begins with a Vigil Mass on Christmas Eve, followed by one at midnight. Other Masses take place on Christmas Day. Local parishes determine the exact number and times of the Christmas Masses, depending on congregational needs. For example, the Vigil Mass often focuses on families and young children. In some places, the traditional "midnight" Mass now begins earlier, perhaps around ten o'clock.

The December 25 date for Christmas was not chosen until the fourth century. Before this time, the anniversary of Christ's birth generally was observed within the context of Epiphany in January. According to the calendar followed in the Roman Empire at that time, December 25 marked the winter solstice: nature's darkest time of the year. Christians used this pagan celebration of the birth of the sun god on that day to celebrate the birth of Jesus as the "Light of the World."

Important feasts in the Church calendar are celebrated for eight days, called an octave. Easter is the most important of these. Christmas has an octave as well. During the Christmas Octave, the Church honors St. Stephen, Christianity's first martyr (December 26); John the Evangelist (December 27); the Holy Innocents (December 29); and the Holy Family (the Sunday between Christmas and January 1).

The Octave Day of Christmas, January 1, has a history of its own. Because pagans in the early Christian centuries spent New Year's Day in riotous festivities, the Church decided to make it a day of prayer in reparation for the excesses. Because of its connection with Christmas, it has always been associated with Mary. It also commemorated the naming and circumcision of Jesus according to Jewish tradition. In 1969, when the Church calendar was reformed, the original observance of the Solemnity of Mary, Mother of God was restored.

While Christmas manifests Jesus' humanity, the Feast of the Epiphany shows forth his divinity, symbolized by the visit and gifts of the Magi, or wise men. In many countries, Epiphany is celebrated on the traditional January 6 date. The United States bishops (with papal approval) have assigned the feast to whichever Sunday occurs between January 2 and 8.

The Christmas Season closes with the feast of the Baptism of the Lord. The date varies, depending on the date for Epiphany. Generally the Feast of the Baptism is celebrated on the Sunday following Epiphany, but occasionally it is celebrated on the Monday immediately after Epiphany. In some countries, the traditional Christmas Season extended all the way to February 2, the Feast of the Presentation of the Lord.

The Baptism of the Lord inaugurates the beginning of Jesus' public life and ministry. The liturgical tradition of the Church sees Christ's divinity manifested in three events from the Gospels: the coming of the magi, the baptism by John and the wedding feast at Cana.

Ordinary Time

The time between the end of the Christmas Season and the beginning of Lent is the first part of Ordinary Time. This can last from five to ten weeks. "Ordinary" is not, in this case, to be interpreted as common or lacking distinction. Rather, the term refers to the arrangement of the succession of assigned Scripture readings for each Sunday's liturgy. A more precise term to describe the system might be ordinal or counted time. Sometimes it is referred to as the Sundays of the year. Each Sunday outside the major seasons is given a number corresponding to the Scripture readings chosen for that day.

For this part of the year, the Gospel readings tell us about Jesus' early ministry of preaching and healing. They also tell us about the call of the disciples. We reflect on our own call as followers of Jesus, and we look at who this person Jesus is.

Lent

Because the date of Easter varies with the lunar calendar used in Jewish tradition to determine the date of Passover, the date for the beginning of Lent, counted forty days back from Easter, also varies.

The first general Church council in 325 decided to celebrate Easter on the first Sunday following the first full moon of the spring equinox. Consequently, the feast can fall on any Sunday between March 22 and April 25. In recent years, however, there has been much discussion on the question of choosing a fixed date for Easter.

Ash Wednesday ushers in Lent. The Gospel reading reminds of the need for prayer, fasting and almsgiving. We mark the beginning of Lent with a day of fast and abstinence. We receive a cross of ashes on our foreheads as a sign of our need for conversion and our willingness to enter into this season of repentance. Going through the day with smudgy foreheads is a visible sign of our faith in the cross of Christ that redeemed us from sin and death.

Many people think of Lent as a time of penance and "giving up" something. While it has a penitential character, it is also a time for reflecting on the baptismal commitment we make as Christians. For the already baptized, it is a time to prepare to renew one's baptismal promises. We seek to follow Christ more closely and pay more attention to spiritual needs. For catechumens, who are preparing for Baptism at Easter, it is the final stage of their journey toward initiation into the Church.

The forty days of Lent draw on biblical symbolism associated with the number forty. For example, in Noah's time it rained for forty days and nights, followed by a time of waiting for the waters to recede. The Israelites wandered in the desert for forty years before reaching the Promised Land. Jesus spent forty days in the desert preparing for his public ministry.

Holy Week

The most solemn week in the entire Church year begins with Passion Sunday. This Sunday also goes by the name of Palm Sunday, because palms are blessed and distributed at the beginning of Mass and we hear the Gospel account of Jesus' triumphal entry into Jerusalem. At the principal Mass that day, the congregation takes part in a procession. The focus of the liturgy is the reading of the Passion from one of the Synoptic Gospels—that is, Matthew, Mark or Luke—as we prepare to enter into Holy Week.

These final days of Lent are spent in even more intense concentration on prayer and sacrifice, like runners in a race giving their all in the final sprint toward the goal. This holiest week culminates in the three most sacred days of the year, known as the Triduum.

The Triduum begins with an evening Mass of the Lord's Supper on Holy Thursday, commemorating the institution of the Holy Eucharist. As a sign of the service Christians are expected to give to others, parishes may have a ritual Washing of the Feet, with the celebrant and representative members of the congregation participating in the ceremony. Some parishes choose to have a Washing of Hands instead, so that the entire assembly can take part. We end with a silent procession in which the celebrant carries the Eucharist (in a vessel called the *monstrance*) to a special repository—either a separate chapel or a side altar in the church. Here the Eucharist remains until the Communion Service on Good Friday. Parishes generally schedule a Thursday evening vigil following the liturgy and lasting until midnight, so that parishioners may spend time in adoration before the Blessed Sacrament.

On Good Friday, we continue the prayer of the Triduum. We begin with no entrance procession or opening rites. The service centers on the reading of the Passion narrative from John's Gospel and on veneration of the cross: symbol of both death and resurrection. A large wooden cross is carried into the sanctuary, and people process forward to venerate the cross with a kiss or another sign of reverence such as a bow or genuflection according to the local custom. We also pray ten solemn intercessions for the Church and the world.

Because there is no Mass on Good Friday, hosts consecrated at the Holy Thursday liturgy are distibuted in a simple rite. Following a simple blessing, the congregation leaves quietly.

The Triduum culminates in the Easter Vigil, the most important solemnity of the year. It is a time of watching in prayer and song and Scripture. Ceremonies begin after dark with the Service of Light. We kindle the Easter fire and from this new fire we light the Paschal candle. The light of the Paschal candle is passed to small candles held by each member of the congregation.

Next comes the Liturgy of the Word. We read as many as seven readings from the Old Testament: the story of creation, the story of Abraham's great faith, the account of the Exodus and readings from the great prophets. We hear Paul's Letter to the Romans, with its teaching on the meaning of Baptism. Finally, we hear the account of Jesus' Resurrection.

In the Liturgy of Baptism that follows, new members are initiated into membership in the faith community through their Baptism and Confirmation. Then, in the Liturgy of the Eucharist, they join the rest of the congregation in receiving Communion.

Christians in the first centuries after Jesus celebrated his Resurrection with an all-night vigil preceding Easter Sunday. Those who had completed the catechumenate received the sacraments of initiation. Over the centuries, the time of the vigil was being pushed back to an earlier hour. In my own childhood, we observed the "vigil" on the morning of Holy Saturday. It was attended mainly by altar servers and choir members, joined by a scattering of the faithful in the pews. The service of light—lighting the Easter fire—occurred in broad daylight, and the blessing of the Easter water was an empty ritual since no baptisms followed. At noon, with the vigil over, the forty-day Lenten fast also ended. That's when we really celebrated!

In 1951, in order to increase attendance at this most solemn liturgy of the Church year, Pius XII gave bishops permission to transfer the morning service to the evening hours. This was done on an experimental basis at first, then made permanent in 1955. Vatican II called specifically for the vigil to take place "after nightfall" and for restoration of the catechumenate—the RCIA. With the initiation of catechumens at the Easter Vigil, this liturgical treasure regained its fullest expression.

The Fifty Days of Easter

The importance of Easter, the most ancient feast in the Church, is signaled not only by the six preparatory weeks of Lent, but also by the extended season of celebration that follows. Like Christmas, Easter has its own octave: eight days of the greatest joy. The season continues until Pentecost.

Nine days before Pentecost, we celebrate the Ascension of the Lord. Ascension Thursday commemorates the end of Jesus' mission on earth. For the remaining days of the Easter season, we prepare for the coming of the Holy Spirit on Pentecost, a day that marks the beginning of the Church's mission of preaching Christ's death and Resurrection.

Ordinary Time Resumes

On the Monday after Pentecost, the Church once again enters Ordinary Time, which extends through summer and autumn, until a new liturgical year begins on the First Sunday of Advent. Each Sunday the Gospel presents a theme based on events in Jesus' life and teachings. In the process, we learn more about our faith and how we should live.

Trinity Sunday, a week after Pentecost, acclaims a God of love. One week after that, we celebrate the Feast of the Body and Blood of Christ (sometimes referred to by its former name of Corpus Christi), when we express gratitude for the gift of the Eucharist.

Through the summer and fall, there are other feasts associated with the Mysteries of Christ. (The word *mysteries* here means all the sacred events and truths that make up the story of our redemption by Christ, from his Incarnation to his anticipated Second Coming.) Some examples: Sacred Heart, in June (changeable date); Transfiguration of the Lord, August 6; Triumph of the Cross, September 14. Additional days honor those who have followed in Jesus' footsteps: saints and martyrs who have lived and died according to gospel values. The Church has a particular love for Mary, both as the mother of Jesus and as a model of discipleship.

Feast Day Celebrations

In the Church calendar, we call the arrangement of seasons and feasts in honor of the Lord the Temporal Cycle; those for Mary and the saints make up the Sanctoral Cycle. The two cycles or divisions run concurrently, with greater weight attached to the Lord's feasts.

Although we think of all these celebrations as feast days, they actually have technical rankings that indicate their individual importance, which in turn determines the degree of liturgical celebration. Topping the list are "solemnities," days of the highest rank, which include Christmas and Easter. Some solemnities honor saints, such as the Birth of John the Baptist, June 24, and All Saints, November 1.

Second in rank are "feasts." In this classification, for instance, are the Presentation of the Lord on February 2 and Our Lady of Guadalupe on December 12.

The last category, "memorials," is subdivided into obligatory and optional. Obligatory memorials are celebrated universally. Two examples are Joachim and Ann (parents of Mary) on July 26 and Therese of the Child Jesus on October 1. Optional memorials, as the name suggests, are celebrated by local communities that have some tie to the saint. For example, the Memorial of St. George (April 23) is usually celebrated by any church named in his honor; St. Jane Frances de Chantal, co-founder of the Visitation Order, is honored on August 18 by religious communities of her order.

Holy days of obligation are solemnities or feasts when the Church requires Catholics to go to Mass. Although there are ten on the universal calendar with this status, a country's bishops can, with Vatican approval, make exceptions to these. In the United States today, there are six such holy days: Mary, Mother of God (January 1); Ascension Thursday (forty days after Easter); Assumption of Mary (August 15); All Saints' Day (November 1); Immaculate Conception (December 8); Christmas (December 25). The bishops have transferred two of the other days to a Sunday observance: Epiphany and the Body and Blood of Christ (Corpus Christi). Two other feasts are still observed on their designated days, but Mass attendance is not obligatory: St. Joseph (March 19) and Sts. Peter and Paul (June 29).

From the early centuries until recent years, the Church calendar also included Ember Days and Rogation Days. (Older Catholics will remember these.) *Ember* comes from an Anglo-Saxon word denoting a regularly recurring time. Ember Days of prayer and penance preceded each of the four seasons, when God's blessings on the harvest were sought. (In the Mediterranean lands where these days originated, harvests could occur in all four seasons.) Similarly, Rogation Days during the Easter Season—three, for instance, before the Feast of the Ascension—asked God's blessing on fields, gardens and orchards. *Rogation* refers to litanies of petition.

Those cyclical practices reflected a time when society was primarily agricultural. Bishops now may institute days of special prayer more in tune with the needs of contemporary society: praying for human rights, world peace or particular local needs. A tradition is waiting to take root here.

Cycles of Readings

Every Sunday in every Catholic church around the world, the same Scripture passages are read during the Liturgy of the Word. Prior to Vatican II, Sunday readings were the same from one year to the next. Now, though, the selections range over a broader, three-year period, consequently covering most of the Gospel material as well as significant portions of the Old Testament. This provides Catholics with a much richer diet of Scripture.

The three years are divided into cycles known as A, B and C. A new cycle begins on the First Sunday of Advent. One of the Synoptic Gospels is read each year—Matthew in Cycle A, Mark in Cycle B and Luke in Cycle C. John's Gospel has a special place on feasts such as Christmas and Easter. John's Passion narrative is always read on Good Friday. We also hear passages from John's Gospel during Cycle B, because Mark's Gospel is shorter than Matthew's and Luke's.

Except during the Easter Season, when we hear from the Acts of the Apostles, the First Reading nearly always comes from the Old Testament. The reading relates in some way to the Gospel theme. The Responsorial Psalm that follows echoes that theme.

On most Sundays, the Second Reading is taken from the letters (epistles) in the New Testament. Ordinarily the passage is not intended to harmonize with the Gospel. Rather, the Second Reading presents the material more or less continuously in order to acquaint the faithful with these writings. For major seasons and feasts of the year, however, the Second Reading may be more directly linked to the Gospel. For instance, in the Second Reading for the Feast of the Holy Family during the Christmas Season, Paul writes in his Letter to the Colossians: "Children, obey your parents in everything, for this is pleasing to the Lord" (Colossians 3:20).

The Gospel is always the focus of the Liturgy of the Word. Through the Gospel readings, we hear and celebrate the life of Christ. Theologians and other spiritual writers refer to this as "unfolding the Mysteries of Christ." For example, on the Feast of the Transfiguration, we hear the story of Jesus' transfiguration on a mountaintop. This revelation of Jesus' divinity represents one of the great truths of our faith.

On weekdays, we hear two readings instead of three. These readings follow a two-year cycle. Year I is followed during odd-numbered years, Year II in even-numbered years. The Gospel is the same in both years, but the first reading varies. It may be taken from the Old or New Testament, and will generally cover an entire book or letter, or a significant story over several days or weeks.

In addition to the readings for Sundays, weekdays and

feasts, the lectionary also includes Scripture passages that may be used at weddings and funerals, as well as for other sacraments celebrated apart from the Sunday liturgy. Participants are free to choose from among these readings for a particular celebration.

Liturgical Colors

We use several colors in liturgical celebrations to strike the mood of the season or feast. Until the ninth century only white was used. White, signifying purity, joy and triumph, is still the color for the most important solemnities and feasts in the Church calendar: the Easter and Christmas Seasons, solemnities of the Lord during Ordinary Time, feasts of Mary, of saints who were not martyrs and of the angels.

Green, the color of hope, life and growth, is traditional for Ordinary Time.

Violet, or purple, worn during Advent and Lent, indicates a time of expectation as well as purification or penance. Purple may also be worn for funeral Masses.

Red is the choice for feast days of the apostles and martyrs, and also for Passion Sunday, Good Friday and Pentecost. It symbolizes sacrificial love for God.

Vestments of gold fabric or other precious materials—expressing triumph and joy—may be an alternate choice for the greatest solemnities.

Black, once worn at funerals as a sign of mourning, may still be worn, but white is more common today to emphasize our faith in Resurrection.

On the Third Sunday of Advent (Gaudete Sunday) and Fourth Sunday of Lent (Laetare Sunday), rose can replace violet as a sign of joy, in anticipation of the approaching feast. (*Gaudete* and *Laetare* are both derived from Latin words for "rejoice"; they are the opening words of the Mass Proper for these days.)

Living According to Sacred Time

Toward late November, as the Church year draws to a close, both Sunday and weekday readings give us prophetic descriptions of the end time. On the final Sunday of the year, we honor Christ the King, the Alpha and Omega, beginning and end for all who are Christian. This solemn feast is a time to celebrate the present, to reflect back and to look ahead to a new Church year.

By journeying with conscious awareness through an entire Church year, we discover the richness it gives to the passage of time. In the process of cultivating the virtues and values appropriate to each Sunday celebration, feast day and special season, we enhance our spiritual growth. Allowing our days to mesh with sacred time makes us aware of the presence of the divine in the rhythm and flow of our lives.

For Further Reading

Bishops' Committee on the Liturgy, National Conference of Catholic Bishops. *The Liturgical Year: Celebrating the Mystery of Christ and His Saints.* Washington, D.C.: NCCB, 1985.

Nelson, Gertrud Mueller. *To Dance with God: Family Ritual and Community Celebration.* Mahwah, N.J.: Paulist Press, 1986.

CHAPTER FOUR

The Seven Sacraments

The sacraments mark key moments in our lives as Catholic Christians. Baptism, Confirmation and Eucharist initiate us into the life of Christ in the Church. Reconciliation and the Anointing of the Sick bring healing to soul and body. Marriage and Holy Orders are a formal commitment to a vocation of service to God and others. Because these rituals are so important to the Church and its members, many customs have developed around them. This chapter will focus more on these peripheral customs than on the theology of the sacraments.

Baptism

Baptism, the first sacrament we receive, initiates us into the faith community. We are reborn as children of God and spiritually purified. Original sin is washed away. When adults are baptized, the sacrament also removes the effects of any sins committed before Baptism.

Baptisms today are often celebrated in the context of a Sunday Mass. For adults going through the Order of Christian Initiation, Baptism takes place at the Easter Vigil. A reception after Mass, welcoming the newly baptized into the community, is becoming more common. In the past, the Rite of Baptism was ordinarily conferred on a Saturday or Sunday afternoon, with only family, sponsors and perhaps a few friends present.

The baptistery in some churches still contains only a baptismal font. In newer churches and some renovated ones, however, a small walk-in pool for adult baptisms is installed. Both baptism by immersion and adult baptisms show a return to the common practices of the early Church. The baptistery may be located near the entryway of the church, symbolizing Baptism as the entrance into the faith community. Or the baptistery might be situated near the altar, linking Baptism to Eucharist and ensuring that the rites celebrated there will be visible to the congregation.

Catholics baptized as infants are often referred to as "cradle Catholics." The Church recommends that babies be baptized as soon as reasonably possible, though timing depends upon variables: severity of weather, distances to be traveled by godparents and relatives, length of the parish's sacramental preparation program. (On average, the latter runs from two to four sessions. The parents—and godparents, if feasible—are expected to attend these sessions, which may be conducted by a parish priest or other staff person.)

While parents are primarily responsible for bringing up a child in the faith, the sponsors, or godparents, ideally support the parents in this responsibility. If circumstances warrant (death of the parents, for instance), godparents should see that the child receives the proper religious instruction and upbringing. Godparents often reinforce and celebrate the spiritual relationship by remembering their godchildren with small gifts on birthdays or baptismal anniversaries.

Only one godparent is required, though two are customary. If two godparents are chosen, one must be male and the other female. A sponsor must be at least sixteen years old and a practicing Catholic who has been confirmed and has received First Communion. A person who belongs to another Christian denomination may take part in the ceremony as a witness but not as a sponsor or godparent.

A baptismal name gives the bearer a model and a patron. Customarily, a saint's name or a name with some kind of Christian association is chosen. Names of virtues—such as Hope, Faith or Grace—fit in with this idea. Names from the Old Testament, too, can provide models of holiness.

A handmade christening gown was a widely popular tradition in the past. Sewn of a fine fabric and elaborately trimmed or embroidered, it often became a family heirloom, handed down from one generation to the next.

In the not-so-distant past, an adult interested in joining the

Church signed up for a series of instructions, given either individually or in a group by a parish priest at the rectory. When a person seemed to have grasped what was required of a Catholic, Baptism took place in a private ceremony.

Today, adults who wish to be baptized participate in a formation process called the Order or Rite of Christian Initiation. Adults receive not only Baptism, but also Confirmation and First Eucharist, the three sacraments of initiation. This had been the common practice in the early Church, and the Second Vatican Council called for its restoration.

Children who have reached catechetical age (seven years) without being baptized generally go through an adapted version of the Order of Christian Initiation rather than being baptized according to the Rite of Baptism for Children.

Baptized Christians from other denominations who wish to join the Catholic Church are not baptized again, although they may receive formation in the Catholic faith together with catechumens. They become candidates for full communion with the Church. When they are ready, they celebrate the Sacrament of Reconciliation, make a solemn profession of faith, are confirmed and receive the Eucharist at a regular Mass. This can also be done at the Easter Vigil.

Confirmation

Confirmation confers on the recipient the graced strength to be an effective witness to the faith through the power of the Holy Spirit. In past decades, entire classes of grade school students were routinely confirmed by the bishop when he made his periodic visitation to the parish. Part of the rite then included his giving the candidate a light tap on the cheek, making one a "soldier of Christ," ready to risk misunderstanding and even persecution for the faith. Older students teased the younger children about the "blow" they could expect to receive, and the more gullible ones steeled themselves for pain.

Today the Sacrament of Confirmation is the subject of

much debate in liturgical and theological circles. In the restored Order of Christian Initiation, it is administered at the same time as Baptism and First Eucharist. The bishops had the task of determining a national policy on the age for confirming "cradle Catholics," but in reality this varies from diocese to diocese, with minimum ages ranging from seven to sixteen.

In many dioceses and among religious educators, Confirmation has been regarded as a sacrament of Christian maturity, an adult commitment to the faith professed by one's parents at Baptism. It signals that the person is prepared to put into practice some form of Christian service. Typically Confirmation classes consist not only of instruction but also participation in volunteer service of some kind, usually connected with the parish or local community.

The sacrament is still administered by the bishop at the time of his periodic visitation. The rite itself takes place during Mass, after the Gospel. The former practice of taking a special Confirmation name, which symbolizes embarking on a new way of life, is now optional.

Penance (Reconciliation)

One of the distinguishing aspects of Catholic life is the practice of "going to confession." In the fairly recent past, long lines in church were common on a Saturday afternoon as penitents waited to enter the confessional box. Conscientious parents would send their children to monthly, if not weekly, confession. Since adults tended to receive Communion less frequently, they might only confess before major feasts. At times the recitation of sins was almost mechanical, what some have called a "laundry list" of sins. People received absolution and a penance, often saying a stipulated number of "Hail Marys" or "Our Fathers." Many Catholics see individual confession of sins as the "sacrament of avoidance," although communal penance services draw a fairly good attendance.

Today's approach reflects a return to a consideration of the social consequences of sin and the need for spiritual healing. Sin separates a person from God and from the rest of the community. The focus of the sacrament is on reconciliation. The penitent's sins are forgiven, restoring a right relationship with God, self and others.

Confession of sin, followed by penance, has been practiced by Christians since apostolic times. When the early Christians realized that even after Baptism a person could fall into serious sin, they had to consider how to reconcile that person to the community again. Serious sin affected the whole community, and public penance was required. Offenders might receive penances that lasted years, even a lifetime; they could not receive Holy Communion during the penitential period.

In the seventh and eighth centuries, Irish missionaries brought the practice of private confession, common in their monasteries, to continental Europe. This practice took hold. The penitent would sit face-to-face with the confessor (priest) somewhere near the altar. The confessional box, which allowed total anonymity, was introduced in the sixteenth century.

In 1215 the Church began to require people to make an annual confession. Today the sacrament is mandatory only when a grave (mortal) sin has been committed. A person is expected to go to confession before receiving Communion again. But many people receive the Sacrament of Reconciliation regularly as a means of overcoming lesser faults and growing in virtue. While not mandatory in the case of minor (venial) sins, confession is still strongly encouraged.

Communal penance services have become commonplace in many parishes in recent years, often taking place during the seasons of Advent and Lent. Celebrating this sacrament as a community reminds us that sin is never a completely private affair. This rite includes hymns, Scripture readings, a homily, guided examination of conscience, an act of contrition or other form of expressing sorrow, praise of God's mercy and a prayer of thanksgiving. If enough priests are available, individual confession follows the communal service. Although the Church provides for a rite of penance with general absolution when the number of penitents far exceeds the number of confessors, its use is discouraged in all but emergency situations.

Children preparing to receive their First Communion are encouraged to make a First Confession before that. By the age of seven, children are considered to have reached the "age of reason"—that is, able to take responsibility for their actions and to distinguish between right and wrong.

Priests are obliged never to divulge what they hear in confession, even if put under oath in a courtroom. This "seal of confession" remains in effect even after the death of the penitent and has an admirable history of being preserved.

The Eucharist

Eucharist is the third and final sacrament of initiation. Repeating Jesus' words of institution at the Last Supper, a priest consecrates bread and wine, the ritual by which the body and blood of Jesus Christ becomes truly present under the forms of bread and wine. This spiritual food and drink nourishes our life of faith.

An important occasion in the life of every Catholic child is the day of First Communion. Second grade, around age seven, is the usual age. First Communion typically takes place in the month of May, during the Easter Season. It has long been the custom for girls to wear a white dress and veil, while boys wear white shirts and dark blue trousers, or sometimes white suits. This has been changing over the past decade or two, but is still expected in some places. Mass may be followed by a First Communion breakfast for children and their parents in the school or parish hall, along with a photo session for the new communicants. Among suggested gifts from godparents or relatives are a rosary, prayer book, religious medal, or shelf-size statue of Jesus or a favorite saint.

Among the changes brought about in the Sacrament of Eucharist following Vatican II were Communion in the hand, Communion under both kinds and lay extraordinary ministers of the Eucharist. In 1977, the United States bishops approved Communion in the hand, a hotly debated issue. Several European countries had already made this change. For several centuries prior to this time, it had been customary for the priest to place the host on the communicant's tongue. The railing that separated the sanctuary from the main body of the church also

38

symbolized the table at which the faithful gathered to share in Communion. It was easier for the celebrant to give Communion on the tongue to a person kneeling at the railing.

The *Constitution on the Sacred Liturgy* had already opened the way for the reception of consecrated wine by the congregation, a common practice in the early centuries of the Church that fell into disuse during the later Middle Ages. Catholics believe Jesus is fully present in either form received, but reception of both the consecrated bread and the consecrated wine mark a fuller participation in the action of the liturgy.

Only a priest may consecrate the sacred elements, but the Eucharist can be distributed by others who have been trained as eucharistic ministers. They perform this function at Mass, and they also take Communion to the sick at home or in hospitals as well as to others who are homebound.

In the not-so-distant past many Catholics only made a "spiritual Communion" rather than actually receiving the host. Some only felt worthy to receive if they had gone to confession the previous day. Others may have broken the required fast. The stringent fast of no food or beverage (even water) from midnight until the time of Communion led to many partaking of the sacrament only on major feasts. In order to encourage more frequent reception of Communion, this stringent fast was gradually reduced, beginning in 1953. Today one must observe a fast for only an hour before the actual moment of reception. Water is permitted, as are medicines. The aged, the sick and their caregivers need fast only fifteen minutes beforehand, and even that is not enforced.

Church law requires reception of the sacrament at least once a year. This "Easter duty" (reception at some time between the First Sunday of Lent and Trinity Sunday) still holds, though most Catholics receive regularly.

Catholics may not take part in Communion services of another denomination, nor are Christians of other denominations permitted to receive Communion at a Catholic liturgy.

Holy Orders

Holy Orders is the sacrament by which a man is consecrated to service in the Church, particularly for sacramental ministry. Holy Orders also grants teaching authority, for example, preaching the Gospel, and the right to exercise pastoral leadership, most commonly at the parish level. A priest may be given additional duties and responsibilities by his bishop or religious superior. The Church teaches that Holy Orders imprints an indelible character upon the recipient's soul, making the sacrament a lifetime commitment.

Deacons, priests and bishops go through ordination rituals that include the laying on of hands and a specific prayer for each order. Acts 6:1-6 describes the laying on of hands when the first deacons were commissioned. From that time on, leadership has been conferred by the imposition of hands.

The hierarchical order of the priesthood developed gradually as the ecclesiastical institution grew and more specialized ministries became necessary. Presbyters (from which "priest" is derived) originally belonged to the council of elders who assisted the overseer (*episcopos* or bishop) of each community.

Deacons were appointed in the earliest days of the Christian community to meet the practical needs of people in the community, leaving the apostles free to preach the gospel. Deacons also began to assist in liturgical functions, for example, the Baptisms of new Christians. Over the centuries, the diaconate eventually became merely a step toward priesthood. Today we refer to this as the transitional diaconate. After Vatican II, the permanent diaconate was restored.

The Rite of Ordination typically takes place in the cathedral of the diocese where the newly ordained will serve. In addition to the laying on of hands and prayer of consecration said by the bishop, a priest is invested with a stole and chasuble (a deacon is invested with a stole and dalmatic). The new priest's hands are anointed with chrism. Usually, more than one priest is ordained at the same time, and they concelebrate Mass with their bishop. A priest traditionally celebrates his first Mass in his home parish.

A bishop is ordained by other bishops. He is anointed on the head, presented with the Book of Gospels and invested with a ring, pastoral staff and mitre—all symbols of his episcopal power. A mitre is a tall hat shaped somewhat like a double cone and is worn for ceremonial occasions.

In a later chapter, we will look at the requirements, training and ministerial functions of deacons and priests.

Marriage

In the Sacrament of Marriage, a man and woman enter into a sacred bond intended to foster their love and promote family life as they commit themselves exclusively to one another. The graces of the sacrament sustain the couple as they build their life together.

A couple intending marriage are expected to contact the pastor of the church where they plan to wed about six months before the anticipated date. (Diocesan policy may vary on how much notice must be given.) Weddings ordinarily take place in the parish church of the bride. In mixed marriages (when one of the couple is not Catholic), the ceremony would normally take place in the church of the Catholic party.

The intervening months allow time to plan the liturgical celebration with the priest. The couple chooses the Scripture readings and music for the wedding liturgy. Many dioceses and parishes have guidelines for wedding liturgies. The Rite of Marriage can take place within or outside a Mass.

Marriage preparation sessions also include premarital counselling, often conducted by a married couple trained in that special ministry. Supportive programs such as Engaged Encounter, a weekend retreat, also offer helpful preparation. Couples discuss their expectations of each other; views on religion, child-rearing and finances; and thorny issues such as extended family celebrations like Thanksgiving and Christmas. Marriage preparation programs help couples understand areas that might cause conflict later.

Canon (Church) law examines issues of capacity, consent and formalities in determining whether a couple can validly marry in the Church. For example, both parties must meet the legal age (fourteen for females, sixteen for males—though such early marriages are discouraged); nothing can prevent a legal union (for example, close blood relationship); both parties must be free to marry and must freely consent to the union. At one time, banns—a public announcement of the impending marriage at Mass on three successive Sundays—were necessary so people who knew the couple could bring to light any existing impediments to the marriage. This practice is less necessary now because impediments will likely be revealed during the period of preparation.

In the past, the non-Catholic party in a mixed marriage had to sign a paper promising to raise the children of the union in the Catholic faith. This is no longer the case, although the non-Catholic is instructed about Catholicism in order to better understand the intended spouse's faith. The Catholic party, however, does sign two statements promising (1) to continue living in the faith, and (2) to pass on that faith to the couple's children through Baptism and subsequent religious education.

In a mixed marriage, a clergyman of another denomination may be present to pray with and bless the couple too. With a dispensation (special approval from the bishop) a wedding can take place outside a Catholic church with a non-Catholic minister officiating as long as a priest is in attendance. The Catholic and non-Catholic ministers would not, however, celebrate the actual ritual together.

In cases where the Church grants an annulment, it has determined that a sacramental marriage never took place. The couple was legally married, according to civil law, but the conditions necessary for a valid sacramental marriage were not present. A legal divorce does not prevent a Catholic from receiving the sacraments, but the person is not free to remarry without an annulment or until the death of the first spouse.

Anointing of the Sick

Vatican II brought to this final sacrament not only a new name but also an understanding closer to that of the early Church. From the twelfth century until the Council, the term "Extreme Unction" or "Last Rites" was used. You might guess, and rightly so, that people dreaded calling a priest to administer to a loved one a rite that by its very name heralded death. The solace and healing graces of a ritual anointing were therefore often lost to the ill person or put off until it was almost too late. On the other hand, people had a great fear of dying without a last priestly blessing. Catholics carried cards or wore medals that read: "I am a Catholic. In case of accident, please notify a priest."

In those days, people were far more apt to die at home rather than go to a hospital. Practically every household was equipped with a sick call set, usually in the form of a crucifix that slid open to reveal a vial of holy water, small candles and a bit of cotton for the anointing.

Anointing of the Sick is the sacrament administered when a person's health is seriously impaired due to illness or old age. Anointing may also be done before major surgery. Even children who are seriously ill can be anointed if they are capable of understanding the meaning of the sacrament. The sacrament may be administered on an individual basis or in a communal setting.

The sacrament channels God's healing graces to comfort and strengthen the faith of the person who is ill. It can help a person endure suffering. In addition to the spiritual benefits, an anointing has positive psychological effects, and sometimes even results in a physical cure.

Healing was an important part of Jesus' ministry, and the apostles continued to heal people in his name. For many centuries, anointing with oil was considered a prayer for healing.

Today, we have one sacrament with two rituals: one for the sick, another for the critically ill or dying. This latter ritual aids the passage from this life to eternal life. Holy Communion given to a dying person is called *Viaticum* ("provision for a journey"). If a Catholic is unconscious or too ill to respond, but those present believe that the person would wish to receive the sacrament, it can still be administered.

For Further Reading

Martos, Joseph. *Doors to the Sacred: A Historical Introduction to Sacraments in the Catholic Church.* Tarrytown, N.Y.: Triumph Books, 1991.

Roberts, William P. *Encounters with Christ: Introduction to the Sacraments.* Mahwah, N.J.: Paulist Press, 1985.

CHAPTER FIVE

Sacramentals

The Church is rich in holy actions and objects that appeal to the senses as well as express a spiritual reality. Sacramentals are a distinctive part of Catholic culture, the "stuff" upon which Catholics thrive. Just as the Church year makes us aware that time is sacred, and the church building reminds us that space is sacred, sacramentals help us to celebrate the sacredness of our everyday lives.

Sacramentals may be used at Mass (candles are an example), in administering a sacrament (anointing with holy oil), in devotional practices (genuflecting before a tabernacle), or in daily life (wearing a religious medal). Sacramentals are not talismans—good luck charms that have magical powers. Rather, sacramentals are to be used in faith for religious purposes. An attitude of reverence is essential.

Sacramentals may be divided into three broad categories: (1) sacred actions, (2) blessings, (3) blessed objects.

Sacred Actions

The most familiar sacred action, dating back to at least the second century, is the Sign of the Cross. This simple and readily identified action is a fundamental profession of faith: By Jesus' death on the cross we were redeemed. The sign contains a wealth of meaning: It marks one's identity as a Christian; the accompanying words ratify belief in the Blessed Trinity; making the sign with holy water renews our baptismal promises.

This sign takes several forms, depending upon the circumstances. The large Sign of the Cross, touching forehead, chest and shoulders, is the most common. We make it upon entering a church or at the start and close of prayers. We make a small sign on forehead, lips and chest as we prepare to hear the Gospel.

During the administration of the sacraments and other liturgical functions, the Sign of the Cross is frequently made. For example, in the Anointing of the Sick, the priest anoints the sick person's forehead and palms by tracing a tiny cross. In extending a blessing, the priest traces a cross in the air. At one stage in the rites for catechumens, lay catechists (religious education teachers) and sponsors, acting as representatives of the faith community, trace a cross on the forehead of the catechumen as a sign of loving welcome.

Sprinkling rites and the use of incense are two familiar sacramentals that take place during liturgical rites. A sprinkling rite can be an alternative to the penitential rite, particularly during the Easter Season. It is also used to bestow blessings, in the Sacrament of the Anointing of the Sick and in the funeral liturgy. The sprinkling rite symbolizes a renewal of our baptismal commitment. (Note how often in sacramentals we renew our baptismal promises.) We use incense to reverence the altar and the Book of the Gospels at Mass, and the casket at a funeral.

Other sacramental actions include the gestures and postures we assume for private or public prayer, for example, kneeling and folding our hands. We may raise our arms with palms extended upward, a prayer position used by ancient Christians that is being revived in some places today.

Blessings

Blessings play an important role in the life of Catholics. The recently issued *Book of Blessings* contains more than two hundred official blessings for liturgical use. The United States Bishops' Committee on the Liturgy has also issued a companion volume, *Catholic Household Blessings and Prayers*, for use by lay Catholics in their everyday lives.

A blessing ritual invokes divine favor to make persons or

things holy or to ask for God's care and protection. Through the great range of blessings available, we can sanctify all aspects of our lives.

In the past, blessings often consisted of a few ritual words and an accompanying action by a priest. Today's ceremonies have been enhanced as a result of the liturgical renewal following Vatican II. A blessing now might include an introductory rite, a Scripture reading appropriate to the blessing, intercessory prayers and the blessing prayer itself. Actions include signing with the cross, sprinkling holy water, incensing or anointing with holy oils. Those present are expected to participate in the blessings and prayers through their responses.

All manner of things or persons in all kinds of circumstances can receive a ceremonial blessing. What follows gives just a sampling.

At the dedication of a new church, both the building itself and the altar are blessed, usually by the diocesan bishop. The ritual includes sprinkling holy water on the walls, the altar and the assembly—the people being the spiritual temple. The walls and altar are anointed with chrism and incensed. Prior to first use, chalices must be blessed; other liturgical vessels and vestments may receive a blessing too.

On other Church occasions, blessings are invoked upon people. The most familiar of these is the Final Blessing the priest gives at Mass as part of the Concluding Rite. Another example is the Nuptial Blessing of the bride and groom, when the presider at the marriage prays "that God will surround this couple with love, with peace, with the strength to be faithful to one another, and to be an example of kindness to all."

For those serving in various parish ministries, we have blessings for altar servers and lectors, ushers and musicians, eucharistic ministers and religious education teachers and many others.

The sacredness of family life gets recognition too: for example, blessings for a mother before and after childbirth, for a couple on their wedding anniversary, for those honored on Mother's or Father's Day, for the homebound elderly. Homes may be blessed, usually by the local pastor. In this ceremony, rooms are sprinkled with holy water and incensed while prayers of blessing are said.

The sacredness and dignity of work is shown in the blessing, sometimes done annually, of agricultural fields and fishing fleets.

Animals too may receive a special blessing, reflecting the worth of all God's creatures. Traditional days for blessing farm animals and household pets are the feasts of St. Anthony of Egypt (January 17) and St. Francis (October 4).

Two time-honored feast days that include blessings are Candlemas and the Feast of St. Blase. The first occurs on February 2, the Feast of the Presentation of the Lord. Since the fourth century, the feast has been marked by a procession of light, commemorating the occasion when Jesus' parents presented the infant at the Temple and Simeon first proclaimed him as the light of the world. The feast is called Candlemas Day because it became customary to bless candles on this day for liturgical and home use.

On February 3, the Church honors St. Blase, a fourth-century bishop and martyr. Legend tells us that he was a physician before becoming a bishop; further, he healed a boy who was choking on a fishbone lodged in his throat. Since the eighth century, St. Blase has been the patron saint of persons suffering from diseases of the throat. At the end of the feast day Mass, people may come forward for a blessing of throats. The blessing is given by a minister (ordained or lay) touching the throat with two candles joined together in the form of a cross, often tied with a red ribbon. The minister prays, "Through the intercession of St. Blase, may God deliver you from every disease of the throat and from every other illness." This blessing reminds us of God's protective love.

Blessed Objects

Certain material objects may be used for public worship or in private devotions. Their sacramental purpose is often made clear through a blessing by a priest or bishop.

Holy water is undoubtedly the best known of these

sacramentals. The use of this water is a constant reminder of our Baptism. Most of the Church's blessings and other rituals use this symbol of new life and spiritual rebirth. During the Easter Vigil, one of the central actions is the blessing of the Easter water. Many Catholics follow the custom of filling a small container with this blessed water for home devotions.

Candles symbolize Christ as the light of the world. They are a mark of reverence and a sign of joyous celebration when used in liturgical services. Candles for liturgical services once had to be made primarily from beeswax. This dates back to a medieval belief in the virginity of bees and thus the purity of beeswax. Beeswax candles are still preferred since they burn better than paraffin candles. Vigil lights can be burned before a sacred image as a sign of reverence and our desire to remain present to God in prayer as we go about the day's business.

Holy oils symbolize spiritual strength. They are kept in a cupboard called an *ambry*. This may be built into the sanctuary wall, hung on it, or located in the sacristy or the baptismal area. Though pure olive oil was always specified in the past, other vegetable oils are now permitted.

The Church uses three blessed oils: (1) the oil of catechumens, used in rites during the preliminary stages of a catechumen's journey toward Baptism; (2) the oil of the sick, used for the Sacrament of Anointing; (3) sacred chrism, used for Baptisms, Confirmations and priestly and episcopal ordinations. Anointing with chrism signifies a fullness of grace as well as dedication to the service of God.

The bishop blesses the oils for use within the diocese at the Chrism Mass during Holy Week. Traditionally this Mass was held on the morning of Holy Thursday, but often it takes place on an evening earlier in Holy Week so that more people can attend. In an emergency, a priest may bless oil to anoint the sick.

Blessed palms are used on Passion (Palm) Sunday to celebrate Jesus' triumph over death. In Jesus' day, palms were carried in procession as a symbol of victory. The Gospels tell us that the people welcomed Jesus into Jerusalem by spreading palm branches in his path. In today's rite, branches of trees native to an area may be substituted for the palm. People often take home branches to adorn a crucifix or a home altar. Old palms should be burned before the next Palm Sunday.

Blessed ashes signify mortality, sorrow and repentance. In the early Church, ashes were sprinkled on the heads of public penitents, and later this came to be standard for all the faithful during Lent. On Ash Wednesday, a priest or lay minister signs our foreheads with ashes saying, "Turn away from sin and be faithful to the gospel," or "Remember that you are dust and to dust you will return." The ashes come from last Palm Sunday's palms, which are burned and ground. Some parishes invite members to bring their old palms to church for a ceremonial burning prior to the beginning of Lent.

Incense has played an important role in religious observances since biblical times. As part of a liturgical service, incensing is a way of reverencing persons or objects. Incense comes in the form of powder or grains made from resinous gums, to which may be added oil of roses or other essences. When burned, the incense gives off a fragrant smoke. The fragrance represents virtue and the billowing smoke signifies prayer rising to God. (Some religious goods stores sell incense in small packets for home devotions.)

Sacramentals for Private Use

The most frequently used objects for personal devotions are rosary beads, Bibles and prayer books, religious medals, crucifixes, icons and statues.

Wearing *religious medals* is an ancient practice. Some of the best known are Sacred Heart medals, the St. Christopher medal for protection of travelers (this medal is often hung on car windshields) and the "Miraculous Medal." This medal can be traced to visions of Mary experienced by the nineteenth-century mystic, St. Catherine Laboure. It includes representations of both the Sacred Heart and the Immaculate Heart of Mary.

Shelf-size statues of Jesus, Mary or a favorite saint are traditional for a home altar or prayer corner. For an outdoor grotto or garden, St. Francis outdistances all others. Images and statues and the blessings and prayers associated with them can draw us closer to Christ and the example of the saints. They remind us to praise God and to implore God's protection.

For Further Reading

Book of Blessings. Official Church ritual book, published by both Catholic Book Publishing Company and The Liturgical Press, 1989.

Bishops' Committee on the Liturgy, National Catholic Conference of Bishops. *Catholic Household Blessings and Prayers.* Available from The Liturgical Press, 1988.

CHAPTER SIX

Mary

One of the major distinguishing marks of Catholicism is the special veneration accorded to Mary, the mother of Jesus. At Vatican II, the Council took the position that attention to Mary should not take precedence over that given to her son. For example, the Prayers after Mass, most of them seeking Mary's intercession, were eliminated. These prayers, led by the celebrant following a low Mass consisted of three Hail Marys, the "Hail, Holy Queen" (text of a hymn to Mary), a prayer that began, "O God, our refuge and our strength...by the intercession of the glorious and immaculate Virgin Mary...," and in conclusion, a prayer asking for the protection of Michael the Archangel. These prayers, in the vernacular, had been instituted by a late-nineteenth century pope for the needs of the Church.

While processions with a statue of Mary carried aloft and May crownings of the Mary statue are more memory than practice now in American churches, grass-roots devotion remains a constant. Explaining the hold Mary has on the Catholic imagination, priest-sociologist Andrew M. Greeley, in his book *The Catholic Myth*, writes: "Mary represents the mother love of God, the great historic Catholic insight that God loves us as a mother loves a newborn babe. Such a notion is so appealing that those who understand it, even dimly and preconsciously, will never give it up" (p. 62).

The poor, the downtrodden and all who suffer feel a special kinship with Mary, who experienced suffering and sorrow in her own life. People seek her intercession not just because of her stature as mother of the Lord, but also for the maternal consolations associated with the mother of Jesus.

Mary Through the Ages

Wall paintings in Roman catacombs, dating from before 150, picture Mary holding the Divine Child. The oldest known prayer to Mary was written in Alexandria, Egypt, in the 200's. In Alexandria, then the intellectual center of Christianity, Roman authorities made the first systematic attempt to wipe out the Church. Predictably, the prayer asks for Mary's protection in adversity and danger. The first known hymn in Mary's honor was composed by St. Ephrem the Syrian, deacon of the Church at Ephesus, sometime in the mid-300's.

In the Middle Ages, homage to Mary in the West became as fervent as it always has been among Eastern Christians. The medieval concept of an all-powerful, judging God created the need for a maternal comforter, and Mary seemed to meet this need. Some of the most famous medieval cathedrals were dedicated to Mary. Chartres and Notre Dame, both in France, are two outstanding examples. Her virtues were extolled in sculptures such as Michelangelo's Pieta as well as in paintings and music. Hymns composed then are still being sung. They include *Salve Regina* ("Hail, Holy Queen") and *Stabat Mater* ("At the Cross Her Station Keeping").

Tens of thousands of parish churches around the world today bear her name or one of her numerous titles. Mary's patronage extends to countries. In 1846, the American Bishops received approval from Rome to name Mary as the official patroness of the United States, under the title of Immaculate Conception. The shrine cathedral is in Washington, D.C.

Saturday came to be the traditional day for giving special honor to Mary, an idea first promoted in the West in Charlemagne's time. The months of May and October are traditionally dedicated to her. On occasion, an entire year is designated a Marian Year (actually a fourteen-month observance). The most recent ran from June, 1987 to August, 1988.

A Scriptural Portrait of Mary

Our portrait of Mary is drawn predominantly from Scripture: from the Gospels (particularly Luke's and John's) and the Acts of the Apostles. At the Annunciation, a pivotal event in salvation history, Mary's willingness to do whatever God asks of her shows her complete trust in God. Although Mary was betrothed to Joseph, the two had not yet begun to live together, and the society of her day did not take lightly an unexplained pregnancy. Nevertheless, she was willing to withstand gossip, censure and the possibility of being put to death to bear her child.

She travels "in haste" to be with her older cousin Elizabeth, who is also to bear a child (John the Baptist). Mary, though surely troubled by her own situation, is ready to fly to the side of her cousin, who had gone into seclusion during her own unexpected pregnancy.

We may think of the events surrounding Jesus' birth as an idyllic Christmas-card scene of shepherds, wise men and a host of caroling angels surrounding the Holy Family in a cozy stable. The reality for Mary, however, begins with an arduous, hundred-mile journey to Bethlehem, either walking or riding a donkey. She and Joseph, like everyone else in their land, had to comply with orders of the Roman occupying power and register in person for the empire's census. After Jesus' birth in an unpicturesque cave, the family is forced to flee to Egypt, becoming refugees in order to escape King Herod's massacre of infants.

Luke's story of the early years tells of Mary and Joseph presenting Jesus in the Temple forty days after his birth, in compliance with Jewish observance. On this occasion, Simeon and Anna prophesy both joys and sorrows for Mary's future. When Jesus is twelve, the family makes a pilgrimage to a Jerusalem festival. He fails to join the caravan for the return journey home, remaining instead in the Temple—"lost" to his parents for three days and giving them only a mystifying explanation about doing his Father's business. Luke tells us, "his mother kept all these things in her heart" (Luke 2:51).

John's Gospel contains two incidents that suggest

something about the nature of the relationship between mother and grown-up son. The first occurs at the wedding feast of Cana when Mary lets Jesus know that their host is running out of wine. In a rather lively dialogue, Jesus tells her that it is no concern of his, but she still says to the servants, "Do whatever he tells you" (John 2:5). Obviously his mother has always been able to count on him, but not by telling him what to do!

Mary must have had to deal with the stress caused by his celebrity status, by family misunderstanding of his ministry, by plots against him. Near the end of John's Gospel, we see her at Calvary, standing at the foot of the cross—Jesus could always count on her too. He makes sure that his disciple will take care of her.

Our last glimpse of Mary comes in Acts. We find her with the rest of the fledgling Christian community, gathered in prayer in the Upper Room, awaiting the coming of the Holy Spirit—another kind of birth, with new uncertainties and challenges.

Mary of Tradition

The Gospels are witnesses of faith, not biographies, so much that we would like to know about Mary and Jesus as ordinary human beings is lost to history. Tradition helps to fill in the gaps. One long-standing tradition maintains that Jesus appeared first to his mother after the Resurrection.

Traditional places tell a story too. The early Jewish-Christian community in Jerusalem preserved the remembrance of certain sites associated with Mary. For example, the Church of St. Anne in Jerusalem's Old City is believed to be built over the site of the house where Mary lived as a child. The present church, dating to crusader times, replaced an earlier church of Mary. Moreover, archaeological evidence suggests that a small oratory, or place of prayer, existed on that spot around the year 200.

According to ancient legend, Mary was born during the autumn Feast of Tabernacles, an important Jewish festival; at age three she was brought by her mother to the Temple to be consecrated to God. One version says her mother educated the girl at home after this. Another says that Mary was left at the Temple to serve the Lord.

Various stories about Jesus, Mary and other figures of note circulated among early Christian communities—at first orally, then in written form. Some collections of stories were eventually accepted as part of the official canon of the New Testament. Others formed part of the "Apocrypha," a name for those books that contained both factual and fanciful accounts. These are sometimes referred to as "pious imagination."

One of the best known of the apocryphal books was the Book of James, written around 150-175. From this source we get the names of Mary's parents, Joachim and Ann. Each of them reportedly received an angelic visitation, assuring them that their prayers for a child would be answered. Another story in the Book of James tells a charming story of the choice of Joseph to be Mary's husband. A number of suitors assembled at the Temple, Joseph among them. All carried rods, or staffs. In an angelic revelation, the high priest had been told that the one whose staff flowered was God's choice for the fourteen-year-old maiden. Of course it was Joseph's that bore blossoms. The Book of James also describes Jesus' birth in a cave.

Though Mary does not appear in the New Testament after Pentecost, two different traditions report on her last years. One purports that she spent those years in Jerusalem; the other contends that she and the beloved disciple John went to Ephesus on the west coast of Asia Minor (modern Turkey) to escape persecutions in the holy city. Among the ruins at the site of that ancient city is the first church ever consecrated to Mary. Some believe it covers the site of Mary's home there. Ephesus also has associations with Luke.

Mary of Private Revelations

Through the eyes of witnesses (also called "visionaries") to her apparitions, we can find additional insight into the person of Mary. These appearances have occurred throughout the history of Christianity. Apparitions to individuals are a form of private revelation; not all those reported are accepted as authentic. The Church investigates thoroughly before making a pronouncement on whether an apparition is genuine. For example, those in Medjugorje, a remote mountain village in Croatia, where apparitions have been claimed since 1981, remain under study. Even after the Church declares that an apparition is genuine, people are not required to believe in it.

Mary's appearances have been primarily to children and young people in recent centuries. Her messages for the world have a common thread: people are to repent, pray and do penance; then, it is promised, peace and conversion will come about. Prayers for the conversion of Russia, for instance, were urged when Mary appeared to three children at Fatima, Portugal, in 1917. Some credit the fall of communism to these prayers.

Her appearances have had such an impact on the faithful that their locations become places of great pilgrimage. Major shrines include Guadalupe, Mexico; Lourdes, France; Knock, Ireland; and Fatima, Portugal. At two of the most-visited shrines, pilgrims are counted in the millions each year (five million at Lourdes and nearly that number at Fatima). Since Pope John Paul II's visit to the Irish shrine at Knock, a new international airport has been built to take care of the increased volume of pilgrims. Before the civil war in Croatia impeded travel, Medjugorje played host to an estimated ten million visitors since 1981.

The Church commemorates some apparitions with special days on the calendar, for instance, Our Lady of Lourdes on February 11 and Our Lady of Guadalupe on December 12.

Marian Feasts

As early as the second century, feasts were celebrated in Jerusalem in veneration of Mary. Eastern Christian communities soon followed suit. The Eastern Church was the first to observe the anniversary of her death, which eventually came to be known as the Feast of the Assumption. By the seventh century, the Church of Rome had five Marian feasts on its calendar.

Three of the six holy days of obligation observed in the United States today are Marian feasts: Solemnity of Mary, January 1; Assumption, August 15; and Immaculate Conception of Mary, December 8.

Other important Marian feasts include the Annunciation, March 25; Queenship of Mary, August 22; Birth of Mary, September 8; Our Lady of Sorrows, September 15; and Our Lady of the Rosary, October 7.

Marian Dogma: Official Teachings

To a large extent, the feasts in honor of Mary reveal what Catholics believe about her. Two of the Church's teachings regarding Mary, though proclaimed officially only in more recent times, were widely held by the faithful long before this. The doctrine of the Immaculate Conception, declared by Pope Pius IX in 1854, teaches that from the first moment of her conception, Mary was free from all stain of original sin. Her Assumption into heaven, body and soul, was declared by Pope Pius XII in 1950. Both beliefs had been marked by feast days arising out of popular devotion for close to 1500 years.

Two other articles of faith proclaimed by the Church (meaning Catholics are expected to believe in them) are the virgin birth of Christ, defined by the Lateran Council in Rome in 649 (but commonly believed before that and written about by Church Fathers such as St. Augustine) and belief in Mary as the Mother of God, another early dogma.

The latter was first proposed about the year 100, and eventually pronounced at Ephesus in 431 by a general Church Council, which met appropriately enough in the Church of Mary. In Catholic understanding, this doctrine does not mean she was the Mother of God from eternity, but that she was the mother of Jesus when he came to earth. The council made the clear distinction that Mary was the "God-bearer" (*Theotokos*) in reference to Jesus' human nature, not to his divinity. Translating the Greek *Theotokos* into Latin as *Mater Dei* ("Mother of God") led to misunderstanding, but the Roman Church retained the title.

Mariology is the study of Mary in relation to the overall plan of salvation. It grew out of a need to explain Mary more fully and clearly in response to criticism during the Protestant Reformation. Even today, people of other faiths sometimes mistake Catholic veneration of Mary as adoration or worship that belongs only to God. But Catholic teaching has always been clear on this. The technical term for adoration of the Divinity is *latria*. The homage paid to the angels and saints is classified as *dulia*—they are regarded as holy and deserve honor and respect. *Hyperdulia* is the highest form of veneration shown to any of God's creatures. This is the term Catholic teaching applies to Mary.

Every age has had its particular view of Mary; so too have individuals. Among her many titles are Virgin Mother, Madonna, Queen of Heaven, Blessed Mother and Mary of Nazareth. She is truly a woman for all seasons, our spiritual mother and the model of discipleship.

For Further Reading

Buono, Anthony. *Dictionary of Mary.* New York: Catholic Book Publishing Company, 1985.

Graef, Hilda C. *Mary: A History of Doctrine and Devotion.* Westminster, Md.: Christian Classics, 1985.

CHAPTER SEVEN

Angels and Saints

The first prayer my parents taught me was the Prayer to the Guardian Angel:

> Angel of God, my guardian dear,
> To whom God's love commits me here,
> Ever this day be at my side,
> To light and guard, to rule and guide. Amen.

In my bedroom they hung the popular picture of a guardian angel hovering close by two children crossing a footbridge. My faith began with trusting that God made sure I was cared for when out of my mother's or father's protective sight.

Guardian Angels enjoy their own feast in the liturgical calendar (October 2). In the readings for this feast, we are reminded: "For God commands the angels to guard you in all your ways" (Psalm 91:11). And Jesus says: "See that you do not despise one of these little ones, for I say to you that their angels in heaven always look upon the face of my heavenly Father" (Matthew 18:10). Catholic tradition has long taught that each person is assigned a personal guardian angel.

Angels receive veneration because of their spiritual nature and because of their special link to God as attendants in the heavenly court. In biblical terminology they are viewed as members of a heavenly host surrounding the throne of God. In the liturgy we pray, "Father in heaven.... Countless hosts of angels stand before you to do your will; they look upon your splendor and praise you, night and day" (Preface to Eucharistic Prayer IV).

The three archangels—Gabriel, Michael and Raphael—formerly had separate feast days, but since the calendar of saints was revised, they share a single one, September 29. This date coincides with the anniversary of the dedication of a Roman basilica to Michael, and in many places is known as Michaelmas Day.

Angelology: The Study of Angels

Belief in angels is belief in the existence of beings who are purely spiritual, though in their mission to earth, they may take on human form. Angels are recognized as coming from God.

The standard classification of angels is owed to an anonymous sixth-century Syrian monk known as Pseudo-Dionysius. His writings include a treatise on "The Celestial Hierarchy." He arranged nine choirs of angels into three groupings: the First Hierarchy—Seraphim, Cherubim and Thrones; the Second Hierarchy—Dominations, Virtues and Powers; the Third Hierarchy—Principalities, Archangels and Angels. References to each of the nine choirs or rankings can be found in various Scripture passages. Angels in the third grouping serve as the link between heaven and earth.

The great thirteenth-century theologian Thomas Aquinas set forth an elaborate doctrine of angels in a "Treatise on Angels" in his *Summa Theologica*, the collection of his chief writings. He arranged angels in the same order as Pseudo-Dionysius.

Angels appear in great works of Christian literature such as Milton's *Paradise Lost* and Dante's *Divine Comedy*. The great psychologist Gustav Jung talked about angels, and a continuing fascination with the subject shows up in the works of such diverse writers as philosopher Mortimer Adler, who wrote *The Angels and Us*, and Billy Graham, author of *Angels: God's Secret Agents*. Books on angels frequently make the best-seller lists of Christian booksellers.

Three of these heavenly creatures are actually named in Scripture: Gabriel, Michael and Raphael. (A fourth, Uriel, appears in Jewish apocryphal writings.) These are classed as *arch*angels, sent on important missions by God. Note that each name ends in -el. In ancient Semitic languages, El was one of the names of God.

Gabriel, "man of God," often serves as the divine herald. In Christian tradition, he will be the herald of the Last Judgment. Luke's Gospel tells us that Gabriel spoke to both Zechariah and Mary to announce the birth of their sons.

Raphael, "God has healed," restored Tobit's sight in the Old Testament (Tobit 11:7-14). He is also identified in the New Testament with the angel who moved the healing waters of the pool near Jerusalem (John 5:1-4).

Michael, "who is like God," was regarded by Jews as a special protector of Israel. For Christians he became a protector of the Church. In the Book of Revelation (Apocalypse), Michael is named as the angel of the sword who defeats Satan (Revelation 12:7). In Christian tradition, Michael is preeminent. A late nineteenth-century pope assigned a prayer to be said to "Holy Michael" in the prayers which then came after every low Mass. Michael was petitioned to "defend us...be our safeguard against the wickedness and snares of the devil."

A Biblical Understanding

There's more to angels than meets the eye. Though Scripture has much to say about them, our understanding may be hampered by imagining a creature in flowing robes with feathered wings sprouting from its shoulder blades. This image appeared in the fourth century as artists attempted to provide a symbolic representation of a purely spiritual being.

Examining biblical encounters with angels may lead us to the conclusion that a thousand words are worth more than one traditional picture.

Both the Old and New Testaments abound in references to angels too numerous to recount here. A few examples will illustrate the ministry of angelic beings. Essentially, they act in the service of God. Their most familiar role is that of messengers to earth: communicating God's will and heralding good news. Our English word *angel* is taken from a Greek translation of the Hebrew word meaning "messenger."

In Genesis 18, the Lord's message to Abraham comes via

three angels appearing in human form. One of them tells Abraham that his previously barren wife Sarah will bear a son despite her advanced age. In Luke's Gospel an angel informs Zechariah that his wife Elizabeth will bear a child. The angel explains: "I am Gabriel, who stand before God. I was sent to speak to you and to announce to you this good news" (Luke 1:19). And of course on the occasion of the Annunciation, Mary learned of God's will for her from an angel.

We find angels at the beginning and end of Jesus' stay on earth: at his birth angels bring "good news of great joy" to the shepherds (Luke 2:10); at the Ascension they promise Jesus' return at the end of time (Acts 1:10-11).

Angels also function as guardians and comforters. More than once, God reassures the Israelites of divine protection during their long journey to the Promised Land: "See, I am sending an angel before you, to guard you on the way" (Exodus 23:20). An angel feeds the despairing prophet Elijah in the wilderness, telling him to "get up and eat. He looked and there at his head was a hearth cake and a jug of water" (1 Kings 19:5-6).

During his earthly struggles, Jesus receives angelic comfort. After the temptations in the wilderness, "the devil left him and, behold, angels came and ministered to him" (Matthew 4:11). Again in the Garden of Gethsemane, "to strengthen him an angel from heaven appeared to him" (Luke 22:43).

In Acts 12:7-10, the apostle Peter is rescued from prison when an angel of the Lord appears "and a light shone in the cell." He had to wake up Peter, telling him to hurry and get dressed, then follow him. Peter believes it is a vision until he finds himself safely outside the prison, having passed the guards without being stopped.

The Saints

Among the traditions that set Catholics apart from other Christian denominations is a powerful devotion to the saints. Catholics pray to the saints in the same way that we might ask a friend or relative to pray for our special intentions.

During the early Middle Ages, when superstitions began to take hold, saints came to be viewed increasingly as mediators between God and humankind. People felt that a chasm existed between them and a rather stern God, so they cultivated private devotions, centered mainly on Mary and the saints. They were more comfortable presenting their needs to these human figures than to a fearsome God.

From that time to this, individuals have had their favorite intercessors or patrons. Patron saints may be officially designated by the Church, but more often the role originates at a grassroots level. Virtually every cause imaginable has its own patron, from physical ailments (eye diseases, St. Lucy) and spiritual needs (retreats, St. Ignatius of Loyola), to special situations (safety of travelers, St. Christopher) and occupations (social workers, St. Louise de Marillac). A complete list would cover pages. Even nations have their own patrons. As described in the previous chapter, the United States claims Mary under the title of the Immaculate Conception, while Mexico has Our Lady of Guadalupe. Canada is under the patronage of St. Joseph and St. Ann.

The reason for a patronal connection is not always clear. Jude, for example, was one of the twelve apostles about whom little is known. Yet he became the "saint of the impossible," the patron of what seem to be hopeless causes or desperate situations. When prayers to him are answered, Catholics may place an ad in the classified section of a Catholic newspaper that says something like, "Thank you, St. Jude" with the beneficiary's initials. This is intended to foster devotion to Jude.

Another example is St. Anthony of Padua. Why is it that one of the outstanding preachers in religious history came to be associated with the recovery of lost objects? St. Anthony of Padua is often invoked when a Catholic misplaces house keys or loses any item, big or small. In this case, legend has it that someone once stole Anthony's book of psalms, but was suddenly overcome with remorse for his deed and returned the book.

Halos for Holiness: The Canonization Process

The Hebrews saw some individuals as set apart, holy ones so obviously dedicated to the service of God and faithful to the covenant that they must be closely bound to God in love. Jewish-Christians of the first century believed that all who belonged to Jesus Christ enjoyed a special relationship with God as "God's beloved." The Apostle Paul concluded that all Christians were meant for holiness, "called to be saints."

Today we understand the term *saint* to refer to a certainty that the deceased person's soul is with God in heaven. In Christian history, martyrs, those who died for the faith, were the first to be honored for their heroic sanctity.

After the era of persecutions ended in the fourth century, a Christian's way of living, rather than dying, became the major factor in determining who should be regarded as a saint, although there have been martyr-saints throughout the history of Christianity.

Sainthood by popular acclaim was the norm until late in the tenth century. In 993 John XV declared Ulric a saint of the Church: the first officially recorded canonization. Ulric had been bishop of Augsburg, Germany, until his death in 973.

In the thirteenth century Pope Gregory IX made approval by the Church in Rome mandatory before a deceased person could be listed as a saint and publicly venerated. Abuses had crept in, such as saints more legendary than real receiving veneration and "saints" being acclaimed due to political pressure rather than heroic virtue. Charlemagne, for example, a man with multiple wives who had a deathbed conversion, turned up on the lists of saints due to political maneuverings.

In the sixteenth century, a special congregation in Rome was created to handle the matter. Known today as the Sacred Congregation for the Causes of Saints, it considers a candidate at three different stages: Venerable, Blessed and Saint.

Before the title of Venerable can be awarded, a petition nominating the deceased must originate with the bishop of the diocese where the person lived or worked, with the candidate's religious order or from some other recognized Catholic group. A tribunal at the local level conducts a formal investigation into the life of the candidate, known now as "Servant of God." If the tribunal's findings are favorable, the results go on to Rome, where the Congregation decides whether this Servant of God is worthy to be in the running for the title of Venerable.

The subsequent investigation is conducted by the Congregation for the Causes of Saints. Until recently, the evidence was presented much like a courtroom trial, with an advocate acting as a defense lawyer on behalf of the candidate and a promoter of the faith (sometimes referred to as the "devil's advocate") whose role was to make certain the candidate's virtues were genuine. Today one official from the congregation presents both positive and negative evidence in the saint's cause. If all goes well, the candidate becomes Venerable and is entitled to veneration but only by individual groups associated with the saint's cause.

Beatification is the next stage. Holiness and heroic virtue continue to be important criteria. The individual's writings are examined and his or her character is examined for moral weakness or unorthodox views. For the candidate to be declared "Blessed" an authenticated miracle resulting from the candidate's intercession with God must be given as evidence. Miracles generally involve physical cures, and medical or other scientific evidence must be submitted. Miracles are seen by the Congregation as an indication of divine approval of the candidate's cause. For martyrs, a miracle is not required for beatification.

After beatification, public veneration is permitted in the region where the beatified lived or by the religious community associated with a candidate.

Before canonization can take place, additional miracles are required: one for a martyr; two for a non-martyr. In special circumstances the pope can dispense with some of the usual procedures in canonization, such as the miracle requirement, and make a papal declaration of sainthood. In most cases, though, only after the Congregation for the Causes of Saints has determined that a candidate is worthy of sainthood, does the pope make a public declaration that the person's life was holy and that the Church is certain that he or she is with God.

How Saints Are Honored

Canonized saints receive a listing in the *Roman Martyrology*, a liturgical book first published in 1584. Entries now number more than five thousand. All the saints commemorated on the Church calendar are listed by day throughout the year. A saint is assigned a feast day, nearly always the date of death—considered the "birthday" into eternal life. Universal public veneration is allowed, and church buildings may be named after the saint.

The number of saints keeps growing, so more than one may be honored each day. Only the more prominent ones are noted on the average religious calendar. Often regional differences determine which saint is to be honored. For example, November 16 lists both Margaret of Scotland, one of that country's most illustrious queens, and Gertrude, a famous German mystic. In Scotland, Margaret would take precedence, while in German churches, Gertrude will more likely be honored.

The Church further categorizes saints according to their state in life. Classifications include martyrs, bishops, doctors, confessors and virgins. The first two are self-explanatory. "Doctor of the Church" is a title conferred on theological writers noted for holiness and heroic virtue. Among the saints with this title are Augustine, Thomas Aquinas, Teresa of Avila and Catherine of Siena. The last two are the only women so recognized; both received the honor in 1970. "Confessor"—a distinction reserved to the early centuries—refers not to one who heard confessions but to a person who had been imprisoned and punished during the era of persecutions. Confessors gave courageous witness to the faith at a time of persecution but were not martyred. Only women may be listed as "virgins." Women once married who later enter religious life are listed as "religious."

The Church has long recognized that not every holy person will be enrolled in the official ranks of sainthood. For well over a thousand years, the Feast of All Saints has been celebrated on November 1.

Mystics and Stigmatics

Often misunderstood, often surrounded by controversy, mystics and stigmatics tend to lead extraordinary spiritual lives—though not all are canonized.

A *mystic* might be described as someone who directly experiences the indescribable, overwhelming, loving presence of God over an extended period of time. (Individuals may have one-time religious experiences of God's presence, but that does not qualify them as mystics.) Mystics are not otherworldly, as is often thought. A true mystic combines prayer and practicality, accomplishing a tremendous amount of good while living on a high spiritual plane. Two such mystics are Hildegard of Bingen and John of the Cross—both of whom are canonized.

The word *stigmata* comes from the Greek for "marks," and refers to wounds a person may bear on hands, feet, and sometimes on the side, shoulder or back. Pain accompanies this condition, and blood may also flow. Bearing the wounds is considered a visible sign of one's participation in the Passion of Christ. It is brought on by a strong emotion of compassionate love while contemplating the Passion. (Some individuals deliberately reproduce the crucifixion wounds of Christ on their bodies, perhaps as a result of misguided asceticism, but they are not true stigmatics.)

A holy person who is a stigmatic may be canonized, but not because of the phenomena of the stigmata. The Church is extremely cautious in matters of this sort. The best-known authentic case of stigmata is that of St. Francis of Assisi. Among the saints and mystics who experienced localized pain but did not have visible wounds were Catherine of Siena and Teresa of Avila.

Saints as Role Models

Individuals of every social status have been canonized: from king (Louis IX of France) and queen (Elizabeth of Hungary) to peasant (Joan of Arc) and beggar (Joseph Benedict

Labre). Saints vary just as much in temperament: from the exuberance of Brigid of Kildare to the sober style of Vincent de Paul. No matter what our personality or position in life, we can find an affinity with one of the saints.

We are meant not only to look up to and pray to the saints but to take them as role models of living gospel values and heroic self-sacrifice. In reading lives of the saints, we discover that they did not start out at the pinnacle of virtue, but grew in sanctity through much effort, giving us cause for hope in our own lives.

We may never have the opportunity to do magnificent things for God. However, one of the most beloved saints in Catholic history, Thérèse of Lisieux, a nineteenth-century French Carmelite, showed us the attainable "little way": responding to every situation, no matter how ordinary or mundane, with love and good intentions. This too can demand self-sacrifice of heroic proportions.

For Further Reading

Cunningham, Lawrence S. *The Meaning of Saints.* San Francisco: Harper & Row, 1980.

McGinley, Phyllis. *Saint-Watching.* Garden City, N.Y.: Image Books, Doubleday, 1974.

Walsh, Michael, ed. *Butler's Lives of the Saints.* San Francisco: Harper, 1991.

Ward, Theodora. *Men and Angels.* New York: Viking Press, 1969.

CHAPTER EIGHT

Prayer

American Catholics, when polled about what's important to their faith life, invariably rank "praying alone" at or near the top of the list. A standard definition of prayer tells us that it is lifting the heart and mind to God. Prayer is a wonderful gift given to us by God—the means by which we make contact with the Divine. Prayer offers us the opportunity to draw closer to the loving presence of the Lord, and to deepen that relationship as time spent in prayer becomes a regular part of our day. Whatever path we take, even seeking the intercession of Mary and the angels and saints, the ultimate aim of prayer is to reach God.

Prayer is typically classified according to the intent of the pray-er: (1) adoration or praise; (2) thanksgiving for blessings received; (3) contrition for sins committed; or (4) petition, asking God for help or favors for oneself or for others. (All four elements are found in the Lord's Prayer taught by Jesus.) Prayers of petition are undoubtedly the most common type. Great need leads us to spontaneous, heartfelt prayer. Prayers of petition demonstrate our reliance upon God for everything.

The prayer life of many people generally consists of familiar *formula prayers* (set words, said alone or with others). For Catholics, the best-known of these are the Our Father, the Hail Mary and the Glory Be to the Father. Teresa of Avila, though she reached the heights of mystical prayer, did not disparage formula prayers. But she taught that they should be said with the greatest devotion. So deeply did Teresa ponder the words, that she could begin the Our Father and not get beyond the second word.

Other prayers we learn by heart—many of them ancient in origin—may include the Apostles' Creed, the Morning

Offering, grace before and after meals, the Act of Contrition and the Prayer to a Guardian Angel.

Many older Catholics also cherish the *Memorare*, a twelfth-century prayer written by St. Bernard of Clairvaux seeking Mary's protective care, and *Anima Christi* ("Soul of Christ"), a eucharistic prayer of devotion from the fourteenth century, written by an unknown author. Both prayers, said in English but known by their Latin names, can be found in any standard prayer book.

Older Catholics are also likely to use "aspirations"—brief prayers marked by intense feeling—such as "My Lord and my God" and "My Jesus, mercy." Aspirations can be prayed in the time it takes to take a breath. (These brief utterances are also known as ejaculations.)

Other prayers include the Acts of Faith, Hope and Charity (or Love); Prayer Before a Crucifix; Come, Holy Spirit; and the Prayer for Peace, attributed to St. Francis. Texts both ancient and contemporary abound for every occasion or circumstance.

A *litany* is a formula prayer usually said by a group rather than an individual. The prayer leader gives an invocation and the congregation responds. For instance, in the Litany of Loreto, which honors Mary, to an invocation such as "Queen of all saints" the group responds: "Pray for us." The typical litany includes a series of four dozen or so invocations, followed by a response. Some of the more familiar litanies are the Litany to the Sacred Heart and the Litany of the Saints.

Through the centuries, the Church has accumulated and preserved a vast treasury of works on prayer. Classics of Christian literature include *Introduction to the Devout Life* by Francis de Sales, *The Interior Castle* by Teresa of Avila, *The Practice of the Presence of God* by Brother Lawrence of the Resurrection and *The Imitation of Christ* by Thomas à Kempis.

There are methods of praying to suit every temperament and every state in life. A person may be drawn to a particular style of prayer on a regular basis, but also try other forms from time to time. Often our style of prayer is determined by the circumstances of our lives. The mother of a large family, for instance, might long to meditate, but until her children are older or grown, she may find that aspirations are more within her reach. Any sincere prayer is an expression of love; one is not better than another.

Meditation, though it uses the intellect, is not study. The aim is to understand and then reflect on the truths of faith as they apply to your own life. Your mind understands these things and your heart awakens the desire to do God's will. Meditation may be done individually or in a group setting. Saints such as Francis de Sales or Ignatius of Loyola have devised highly structured forms of meditation, but more simplified forms are also available.

Praying with Scripture has long been part of the Church's tradition. Monastics use the term *Lectio Divina* (Latin for "Sacred Reading") for this form of prayer. At first glance it seems identical to meditation, but it is more contemplative in nature—more "heart" than "head."

Contemplation refers to a type of prayer that consists primarily of resting in the loving presence of God. Types of contemplation "techniques" include Centering Prayer, Prayer of the Heart, Prayer of Quiet and the Jesus Prayer. The Jesus Prayer ("Lord, Jesus Christ, have mercy on me, a sinner") is scripturally based: Bartimaeus speaks these words just before Jesus heals him of blindness (see Mark 10:46-52). In the early centuries of Christianity, the Desert Fathers and Mothers advocated using the Jesus Prayer, and this ancient Eastern tradition has become popular in the West in recent times.

Spiritual exercises make more use of the imagination than other forms of prayer. Those devised by St. Ignatius of Loyola are the best known and most widely used. In fact, most similar exercises are based on the Ignatian method. Although a product of the sixteenth century, the Ignatian exercises have proved adaptable to every age and person.

A formal program of Ignatian exercises may be offered at retreat centers and houses of prayer. Typically, a participant would spend an hour each day in prayer in addition to following a series of prescribed meditations. A participant would see a spiritual director for guidance on a regular basis. The Ignatian meditations are designed for a four-week period, each week having its own spiritual focus, but they can be adapted to a longer or shorter period of time.

Charismatic prayer was strong in the infant Church, beginning with the experience of Pentecost. The tradition was renewed in the United States, beginning in 1967 at Duquesne University in Pittsburgh. The Vatican estimates that the Catholic Charismatic Movement has thirty million adherents worldwide.

"Charismatic" refers to the charisms, or spiritual gifts of the Holy Spirit. Among these gifts are healing, prophesying and glossolalia, or "speaking in tongues" (see 1 Corinthians 12:4-11). Charismatics speak of being "baptized in the Spirit"—being open to whatever direction the Holy Spirit might lead them.

The charismatic form of prayer centers around a weekly prayer meeting that usually includes Scripture readings, hymn singing and periods of silence, as well as spontaneous prayer. Participants share with each other how God is working in their lives.

A *retreat* is a period of time (from a few days to as long as a month) set apart from usual pursuits to give attention to one's spiritual well-being. St. Ignatius began the modern style of retreats some four hundred fifty years ago. However, the Christian idea of drawing apart for a while goes as far back as the example of Jesus, who often took time away from his ministry to pray and spend time with God. Though the broad aim of a retreat is a deepening of faith, it may focus on specific needs such as preparation for marriage or discernment in making an important decision (for example, about a vocation to the religious life).

Retreats are traditionally conducted at centers established expressly for that purpose. You can make a retreat with a group or by yourself. Individual or private retreats at these centers can be self-guided or with the aid of a spiritual director. For first-timers a group retreat is probably the best. The schedule usually includes daily Mass, periods of prayer, solitude and silence, spiritual exercises done under the direction of a priest or another person trained in the field, and spiritual conferences or talks. Time may also be allotted for individual consultation with the retreat director.

Priests and those in the religious life are expected to make an annual retreat. Retreats are also popular with the laity. Parishes often arrange for weekend retreats for their interested parishioners at local retreat centers. The *Catholic Almanac* lists addresses of "Houses of Retreat and Renewal" according to state. For those unable to attend a formal retreat, books and tapes are available for making a private retreat at home.

Liturgical Prayer

The Church's cycle of daily prayer is called the Liturgy of the Hours. This public prayer is part of the official liturgy of the Church, along with Mass and the sacraments. Before Vatican II, it was known as the Divine Office (*Officium divinum*). For the clergy and some religious orders, daily recitation of the Liturgy of the Hours is obligatory. Many laypeople have begun to pray all or parts of this prayer as well.

The service for the Liturgy of the Hours consists of hymns, prayers, psalms and other Scripture passages, along with readings from works of the Church Fathers, the documents of Vatican II and lives of the saints. In a monastic community, the Liturgy of the Hours finds its fullest expression. The monastic life-style makes it possible to pray together at each of the canonical hours (prayer hours through the day, set by canon, or Church regulation). The "hours" are the Office of Readings, Morning Prayer, Daytime Prayer (scheduled mid-morning, mid-day and mid-afternoon), Evening Prayer and Night Prayer. Busy clergy and religious may choose to pray just one of the Daytime Prayers, and the Office of Readings may be recited at any time of day. Often they recite the prayers privately to accommodate their daily activities.

The liturgical reforms of Vatican II once again encouraged the laity to join in this ancient tradition, emphasizing Morning Prayer (the Latin name *Lauds* means "praise") and Evening Prayer (Vespers or "evening star"), the two "hinge" hours in the daily cycle. In Morning Prayer, we praise God for a new day. Evening Prayer is a time to give thanks for the day that is ending. Some parish churches schedule Morning or Evening Prayer services on Sundays or feast days, during the seasons of

Advent and Lent or at other times of the year.

Several versions of the official Liturgy of the Hours are available. *Christian Prayer* is a one-volume edition of Morning and Evening Prayer for the entire year. The *Office of Readings* is sold as a separate volume. The four-volume *Liturgy of the Hours* includes texts for the complete cycle of canonical hours, divided according to liturgical seasons. Check your local religious bookstore for these volumes.

For Further Reading

Hutchinson, Gloria. *Six Ways to Pray From Six Great Saints.* Cincinnati, Ohio: St. Anthony Messenger Press, 1982.

Knight, Fr. David M. *An Armchair Retreat.* Huntington, Ind.: Our Sunday Visitor, 1987.

Pennock, Michael Francis. *The Ways of Prayer: An Introduction.* Notre Dame, Ind.: Ave Maria Press, 1987.

Taylor, Mary Sue. *Prayer for Daybreak and Day's End* (two-volume set). Cincinnati, Ohio: St. Anthony Messenger Press, 1993.

CHAPTER NINE

Devotions: Popular and Eucharistic

Devotions are grassroots rituals. They appeal to people as a way to express their personal religious feelings. From the time of the Middle Ages onward, they have been an important part of our Catholic tradition. When the official liturgy was inaccessible to common people, popular devotions offered spiritual comfort and an expression of fervor and piety.

Since Vatican II, with the Mass, the sacraments and the Liturgy of the Hours being celebrated in the vernacular, the faithful are once again able to enter into active participation in the liturgy. The *Constitution on the Sacred Liturgy* emphasizes that the liturgy is the summit of Christian worship. The purpose of all other devotions is to lead the faithful to closer union with God in the liturgy. Devotions should not be ends in themselves but should encourage people to reach out to others as a way of expressing their love of God.

People in every era hunger for personalized means to say what is in their hearts. Some devotions satisfy a need at a particular time or in a particular part of the world. Others enjoy a perennial and universal appeal. Devotions that have been adapted to every time and place include the Rosary, Stations of the Cross and novenas.

The Rosary

Rosary beads—symbolically, a garland of roses—are distinctively Catholic. In this very popular devotion, pray-ers keep count of prayers by moving their fingers along the beads (sometimes described as "telling" the beads). Praying with beads is an ancient tradition in many religions. From Hindus in the Far East the idea spread to Muslims in the Middle East who use a string of beads to pray the "ninety-nine beautiful names of God." Eastern Christians may have gotten the idea from them. By the twelfth century, in the era of Crusades, the use of beads took hold in Europe.

The laity wanted to imitate the monks who prayed the Psalter—the one hundred fifty Psalms of the Bible. Since most people were illiterate, they substituted the Our Father for the Psalms, using beads to keep count. As devotion to Mary gained strength, one hundred fifty Ave Marias (repeating the Angel Gabriel's greeting to Mary at the Annunciation) were said instead. By the thirteenth century, they added the second half of the prayer now known as the Hail Mary. Through the efforts of the Dominican order, the rosary became a widespread devotion.

In praying the rosary, it is customary to meditate upon "mysteries"—specific events—in the lives of Jesus and Mary while reciting the prayers. Three traditional sets of mysteries —joyful, sorrowful and glorious—add up to one hundred fifty Hail Marys. A string of beads is divided into five decades; one circuit covers one set of mysteries. Suggestions for reflections on the various mysteries are found in many prayer books. Pray-ers may also choose other Gospel events or aspects of faith for meditation.

Stations of the Cross

The Stations of the Cross also have a long history. One legend says that Mary herself revisited the sites associated with Jesus' passion and death. Early in the fourth century, St. Helena (mother of the Roman Emperor Constantine) went on a mission to the Holy Land to verify the sites important in the life of Jesus. After that, churches and shrines were built over them to mark the way for future pilgrims.

Retracing the footsteps of Jesus on his way to crucifixion became a "must" for every pilgrim visiting Jerusalem. In the Middle Ages, crusaders returning home from the Holy Land brought with them the devotional practice of the Way of the Cross, which was accomplished by setting up images depicting the stations (from the Latin *statio*, meaning a "halting place") of Jesus as he journeyed to the cross. In the fourteenth century, the Franciscan Order was given custody of Holy Land shrines (a privilege Franciscans still possess). It is customary today for Franciscans to lead pilgrims along the Way, through the streets of Jerusalem's Old City, each Friday. Through their work in missions around the world, Franciscans popularized the idea of the Stations as a devotion.

The number of stations varied at first, but St. Leonard of Port Maurice, in the eighteenth century, fixed the number at fourteen. Most of them are based on events recounted in the Gospels. The remainder come from legendary accounts, such as Veronica's wiping the face of Jesus with her veil. Today churches often add a fifteenth station—that of the Resurrection— to emphasize that death is not the end of the story, though a reflection on this can also be incorporated into the meditation on the fourteenth station.

Although churches are not required to have stations, nearly all churches have a set on their walls. Only small wooden crosses are necessary to mark the Way for the devotion, but generally stations will be represented by sculpted or painted scenes. While frequently done communally, especially on the Fridays of Lent, the devotion may be prayed on an individual basis, and at any time, in any place, with the aid of a prayer book or other guide.

Novenas

A novena (from the Latin for "nine") consists of nine successive days of prayer for a special intention, which may be for temporal or spiritual needs. The significance of nine is traced to the tradition that Mary and the disciples spent nine days in continuous prayer between the Ascension of the Lord and the coming of the Holy Spirit at Pentecost. Continuous prayer underlines the importance of persevering in prayer.

Novenas can be made individually or in a group. In addition

to the daily prayers of petition, it is recommended that the novena-maker attend Mass and receive Communion frequently during that period, daily if possible. Booklets, and sometimes prayer books, contain texts for popular novenas made to Jesus, Mary or the saints. Among the best known are those to the Sacred Heart of Jesus; Our Lady of Perpetual Help; Jude, Saint of the Impossible; and St. Anthony of Padua, the Wonder-Worker.

If a petition is granted, it is suggested that some form of acknowledgment be made. In the case of favors received through the intercession of St. Anthony, for example, there is a tradition of giving alms—"St. Anthony Bread"—in thanksgiving.

As part of their devotional program, some parishes sponsor a perpetual novena, which entails a prayer gathering of interested parishioners on a specified day each week throughout the year. A parish may also choose to make a novena as preparation for the feasts of Christmas, Pentecost or the Immaculate Conception.

Other Popular Devotions

Devotions vary in degrees of popularity. Some have faded into history now. Others, though less practiced than previously, are still revered and may be observed especially by older Catholics. Here and there, some are being revived.

Devotion to the Sacred Heart pays homage to Jesus' redemptive love. Although not a new idea, the particular form of this devotion began after revelations to St. Margaret Mary Alacoque, a seventeenth-century French nun of the Visitation Order. The Visitation founders had instituted their own brand of devotion to the Sacred Heart within the order; shortly before the revelations, a French priest, John Eudes, founded an order that celebrated a feast in honor of the Sacred Heart. A Solemnity of the Sacred Heart is now observed in the liturgical calendar on the Friday after the Feast of the Body and Blood of Christ.

Among the revelations given by Christ to St. Margaret

Mary was the promise to bless any home in which a picture of the Sacred Heart receives honor. This gave rise to a home-based devotion of "enthronement" (prominent display) of the picture of Jesus with a visible heart and an act of consecration to the Sacred Heart by the family.

St. Margaret Mary also reported that Christ asked that reparation for sin be made by the faithful on the *First Friday* of every month. The resulting devotion consists of going to Mass and receiving Communion on nine consecutive First Fridays in honor of the Sacred Heart. (First Fridays may be kept year-round.) This also led to the custom of priests taking Communion to the sick in their parish on First Fridays. In recent years, lay eucharistic ministers have continued this practice in parishes where the priests are unable to get to all their parishioners.

First Saturdays, begun after Mary's appearances at Fatima in 1917, are of more recent origin, but never achieved the popularity enjoyed by First Fridays. This devotion called on the faithful to receive Holy Communion on the first Saturday of each month for five consecutive months. Recitation of the rosary and confession are also recommended.

The Angelus serves both to pay homage to the Incarnation and to venerate Mary. It gets its name from the opening verse-prayer: "The angel of the Lord declared unto Mary, and she conceived of the Holy Spirit." The Angelus consists of three short verses, with a Hail Mary after each, and concludes with a brief prayer. The text is found in most prayer books.

When the devotion originated in the Middle Ages, it was said each evening for the intention of peace. A fifteenth-century pope specified that the intention be for the protection of Christendom from the Turks at a time when the Ottoman Empire was threatening Europe. The Angelus became a "call to prayer" signaled by ringing church bells at 6 a.m., 12 noon and 6 p.m. Even after the Ottoman threat ceased, the faithful customarily paused wherever they were and knelt in prayer at the appointed hours. This custom diminished as industrialization replaced an agricultural economy.

Some parish churches still toll bells at the designated hours. Today the bishops have encouraged people to pray for peace each noon, a modern adaptation, perhaps, of the Angelus.

Tre Ore (Three Hours) commemorates the three hours Jesus hung upon the cross. The custom originated in Lima, Peru, in the eighteenth century and spread quickly to other parts of the world. On Good Friday, from noon to 3 p.m., parish churches may schedule a service of prayer, hymns and extended periods of silence following reflections given on the "Seven Last Words" (the seven utterances of Jesus from the cross as recounted in the Gospels).

Eucharistic Devotions

Eucharistic devotions include Benediction of the Blessed Sacrament, Forty Hours' Devotion and the Holy Hour. These practices arose in the centuries when frequent reception of Communion was not the norm. The laity turned to devotions focusing on a ritual show of adoration for the Blessed Sacrament. They felt that looking at the consecrated host provided them with spiritual nourishment. It also reaffirmed their belief in the real presence of Christ in the sacrament at a time when Protestant reformers vocally opposed that belief.

In each of these eucharistic devotions, the host is exposed on the altar. People entering the church, especially older Catholics, often follow the custom of a double genuflection (getting down on both knees to show a greater degree of reverence). An ordinary genuflection is sufficient however.

Prior to Vatican II, *Benediction* (from the Latin for "to bless") was one of the most frequently held devotions in every parish. Benediction was common after the Sunday morning High Mass; if there were Sunday afternoon devotions such as Stations of the Cross, Benediction would be featured. It also served as a solemn conclusion to other services.

The sacred host is placed on the altar in a vessel called a monstrance (from *monstrare*, "to show"). The vessel is typically gold-plated, in a sunburst design, and mounted on a stem and base. A transparent circle in the center of the sunburst allows the host to be viewed for adoration. To hold it securely, the host is first placed in a small receptacle, crescent- or circular-shaped, called a luna or lunette. This slides into the "window" of the monstrance.

The priest or deacon incenses the monstrance while the congregation sings the hymn *O Salutaris Hostia* ("O Saving Victim"). Older Catholics often know the Latin by heart, though English is an option. Since Vatican II, any solemn exposition must include a reading from Scripture. Then comes a second incensing, along with the singing of *Tantum Ergo* ("Come adore this wondrous presence"). The words of both hymns were composed by St. Thomas Aquinas.

The high point of Benediction occurs when the priest raises the monstrance aloft, tracing the Sign of the Cross with it, blessing those in attendance. Here everyone kneels in silent adoration. Then the Divine Praises are recited in the form of a litany. The praises are intended to make reparation for blasphemy and profanity.

The ritual ends when the priest takes the host from the monstrance, replaces it in the tabernacle, and the final hymn is sung.

The celebrant wears two special vestments for eucharistic devotions. Over the alb, he wears a cope (a semi-circular cape with hood attached, draped back like a deep collar). This vestment may be worn for special celebrations outside of the eucharistic liturgy. When the blessing is given, a humeral veil is placed over the shoulders and clasped in front of the chest. The long (eight feet or so) silk fabric in white or gold is draped over the hands when the monstrance is held, as a sign of reverence for the Blessed Sacrament. The humeral veil is also worn whenever the monstrance is carried in a eucharistic procession.

Forty Hours Devotion is solemn exposition of the Blessed Sacrament that continues around the clock for forty hours, signifying the hours Jesus spent in the tomb, from his death on Good Friday until the Resurrection on Easter Sunday morning. Early Christians observed a fast during that period. In the sixteenth century, when the city of Milan, Italy, experienced great disaster, people began gathering in churches at different times of the year for forty-hour stretches during exposition of the Blessed Sacrament to pray for divine help. This served as the model for an eighteenth-century devotion, the purpose of which was to make amendment for excesses that took place during the carnivals preceding Lent.

Forty Hours in more recent times was widely popular in the United States. Each diocese assigned its parishes a time during the year for the devotion, so that somewhere in the diocese, at all times, people would be gathered in adoration of the Blessed Sacrament. Parishioners would take turns around the clock keeping vigil. Flowers and lit candles filled the sanctuary. The vigil might also include meditation, prayers and perhaps preaching. The devotion would conclude with a eucharistic procession in which altar servers incensed the monstrance as it was carried through the church by the celebrant. Benediction closed the Forty Hours. In some parishes today, this devotion is seeing a rebirth.

The *Holy Hour* is an hour's vigil before the exposed Blessed Sacrament, again concluding with Benediction. The hour reminds us that Jesus asked his disciples at Gethsemane to watch with him for just an hour.

For Further Reading

Jungmann, Josef Andreas, S.J.. *Christian Prayer Through the Centuries*. Mahwah, N.J.: Paulist Press, 1978.

CHAPTER TEN

Catholic Practices: Minor and Major

Some religious practices—such as going to confession or giving special honor to Mary—have long been synonymous with being Catholic. These observances are deeply rooted in the most essential teachings of our faith. Other Catholic practices, though at one time strongly entrenched, disappear when they are no longer relevant to the times.

For example, in the 1960's, the question of women no longer wearing hats to church was hotly debated. (The "Letters to the Editor" in Catholic publications of that era often reflected the heat of the debate!) Women had been expected to wear a hat to Mass as a sign of respect. When hats were no longer the fashion, and women no longer wore them as a matter of course, they found themselves scrambling for something to put on their heads before they entered a church, even if it was a handkerchief. In time, this practice became obsolete.

Catholicism does not exist apart from the world, and social or political circumstances can have a marked effect on religious practices. In the United States, the Catholic school system took hold in the nineteenth century because public schools were dominated by a distinctly Protestant culture. Prevailing views were frequently anti-Catholic. To preserve their children's faith, a large percentage of parishes around the country set up their own schools. Catholic students were expected to attend their parochial school. Depending upon the dictates of the local bishop, parents could obtain permission to send their children to a public school.

As Catholics began to enter the mainstream of American society in both economic and social terms—an achievement attributed to their overall high level of education—mandated attendance at Catholic schools disappeared. It helped that anti-Catholic sentiments faded too.

Not only were Catholics required to attend Catholic schools, they were also expected to go to Catholic hospitals when they needed medical attention and be buried in Catholic cemeteries when they died.

The laity's liturgical role in the past can be easily summarized. Members of the Holy Name Society (men only) assembled in the front pews on the monthly Holy Name Sunday in order to receive Communion as a body. Some of these men also served as ushers, showing people to their seats, taking up the collection and passing out bulletins after Mass. Women parishioners automatically became members of the parish Altar Society, handling matters such as the laundering of altar linens, cleaning the sanctuary and providing flowers for the church. Several women friends in their seventies, who have now attained their life's dream of serving as readers and eucharistic ministers, tell me that the good old days were not all that good!

Penitential Practices

Penitential practices of various kinds have always registered strongly in the Catholic psyche. From earliest times, Friday has been a penitential day, recalling Christ's sufferings on Good Friday. Until the 1960's, a definite mark of Catholic identity was eating fish on Friday. (Church law actually mandated abstinence from meat.) Catholics quite proudly saw themselves as "good" Catholics with that visible act of self-denial. Restaurant menus in Catholic cities reflected the regulation.

The revised Code of Canon Law, while maintaining that all Fridays of the year are days of penance, left the manner of that penance to national conferences of bishops. In the United States, abstinence from meat is required only on Ash Wednesday and the Fridays of Lent. This is binding on anyone fourteen years of age and older, unless reasons of health excuse a person. On Fridays throughout the year, the faithful are required to do some sort of personal penance or acts of charity.

Fasting has always been a valued practice among Catholics. Its roots go back to Jesus' fasting for forty days before starting his public ministry. In the apostolic Church, prayer accompanied by fasting constituted the twin approach to important undertakings. For the young Church, all Wednesdays and Fridays were fast days; what people saved by fasting was shared with the poor. Later, Church regulations called for fasting during the forty days of Lent and before designated feasts, as well as on the Ember Days occurring in each of the four seasons of the year.

Fasting rules today require that those between the ages of eighteen and fifty-nine limit themselves to one full meal daily (it can be eaten either midday or evening), and two lighter meals sufficient to maintain one's strength. A person may be excused from fasting for reasons of health or other serious problems. In 1966, mandatory fast days were reduced to just two per year—Ash Wednesday and Good Friday. Voluntary fasting, coupled with acts of charity, is the emphasis now. This should be done with a joyful spirit, and not for the sake of appearing pious (see Matthew 6:16-18). In taking personal responsibility for choosing some type of penance, a person might decide to fast from alcohol, tobacco, television or other pleasures instead of food. Fasting is not meant to be life-denying, but rather to be understood as freeing one from worldly attachments, at least for a time.

Many people regard fasting as a very appropriate practice for the times. For in addition to serving as a form of prayer (fasting for peace or other worthwhile causes), fasting has particularly strong symbolism in a consumer society. It reminds us that the resources of the planet ought to be used wisely. Abstinence from meat is also a way of showing respect for creation. Besides being good for the soul, fasting clears the mind and may be beneficial to physical health if not done to extremes.

Offerings can be penitential in nature (a giving up of something), or a presentation of sorts (a giving to someone). Several examples of offerings are listed below.

The spiritual bouquet: One of the loveliest Catholic

customs in the past (still practiced by a relative few) is that of the spiritual bouquet. This is an entirely personal spiritual gift, which may be made up of an assortment of Masses, prayers and devotions, good works and acts of self-denial. To create the bouquet, the gift-giver purchases or makes a decorative card on which are listed any or all of the above. For example, you might offer the recipient the graces of all Masses you attend during a particular month.

A spiritual bouquet is a sign of caring, a highly individualized way of praying for the recipient's welfare or special intentions. A bouquet may also be offered in remembrance of a person who has died. In that case, the card would be given to a relative of the deceased.

In my childhood, spiritual bouquets were a token of affection that children would give to their parents on a Mother's or Father's Day. This impressed the value of spiritual gifts upon formative minds.

"Offering it up": Many older Catholics recall being told to "offer it up" in regard to any kind of suffering or even mild discomfort. A misunderstanding of this led to the mistaken notion that it was good to suffer. We never look upon suffering as a good in itself, but we believe it can be transformed into a kind of prayer by uniting our suffering with Christ's and anticipating resurrection to new life through spiritual growth. Bearing pain with courage and fortitude, rather than turning inward and growing bitter, gives spiritual meaning to what otherwise would be senseless suffering. What is more, it can provide hope and inspiration to others.

Mass card: This card tells the recipient that a Mass will be offered for the person's intention. The card is usually obtained through the parish office, although some religious orders make them available too. The card is usually filled out by the parish secretary, giving the name of the person for whom the Mass is to be offered, the name of the donor, and possibly the celebrant's name and the date on which the Mass will be said. A free-will offering (once referred to as a stipend) is customary. This should *never* be understood as buying a Mass. It is not payment for services rendered. (If uncertain about the amount to donate, ask the church secretary the range in which people usually give.)

A Mass card may also be offered as a memorial to the family of a deceased person in place of, or in addition to, flowers or other remembrances at a funeral.

Observances Associated With a Death

A vigil for the deceased: It has long been customary to observe a vigil on the evening before a funeral by recitation of the rosary, either at the funeral home where the body lies in state or in the parish church of the deceased. The older tradition of the vigil or "wake" is also being restored. The family and friends of the deceased keep watch in prayer as a means of mutual support in their grief. The vigil service is a liturgical rite that emphasizes Scripture readings that offer comfort and hope. A homily, hymns and prayers of intercession, as well as an opportunity for those gathered to offer memories of the deceased are also part of the vigil. Either a rosary or a vigil service or both can be offered, according to the wishes of the family.

Many parishes hold a reception (sponsored by the family or parish friends) after either the vigil or the funeral itself as an occasion to offer words of condolence and to share memories of the deceased.

The funeral: "Mass of Christian Burial" is the preferred term for a funeral Mass. Family members are playing a more active role these days in planning the Mass: working with their priest in selecting Scripture readings and hymns and choosing relatives or friends to be readers, to bring up the gifts of bread and wine and to be eucharistic ministers. Once the Prayer after Communion has been said, relatives or friends may be invited to speak, recalling memories of the deceased as a very personal eulogy. The funeral homily more properly focuses on the Christian hope of resurrection.

Catholics are no longer required to be buried in a Catholic cemetery, nor is cremation now forbidden by the Church. In a non-Catholic cemetery, the burial plot can be blessed beforehand or at the time of the graveside service, when the prayers of committal are said. After the graveside ritual, it is customary to call and offer condolences at the family home or at a reception at the parish. While flowers, Mass cards or other memorials continue to be the typical remembrances, some people prefer to give a financial offering to help with burial expenses.

Remembering the departed: Deceased Catholics have their own feast—All Souls' Day on November 2—and most parishes also remember and honor them during the entire month of November. At Catholic cemeteries, Masses are celebrated on All Souls' Day. Most parish churches provide members with special envelopes on which they are invited to write the names of the deceased whom they wish to remember at all the Masses in that church during November. An offering is typically enclosed, though not required.

The envelopes might remain near the altar throughout the month, or a side altar may be arranged in remembrance of deceased members, perhaps with a scroll inscribed with the names of those who have died within the past year. Some parishes keep a "Book of All Souls" in which parishioners write the names of departed loved ones, and this book is given an honored place in the church during the month. On an individual basis, relatives and friends may visit the cemetery to clean and decorate the grave with flowers on the anniversary of death, special days in the life of the deceased such as birthdays or anniversaries, or near Memorial Day.

All Souls' Day was first observed as a feast in 998 by a monastic order for its deceased. Within several centuries, it had become a universal feast. Since 1915, priests have been allowed to celebrate three Masses on that day. The privilege reportedly came about because Pope Benedict XV was so saddened by the countless soldiers being killed in World War I.

Processions

The ritual of a procession extends thousands of years back in time. Among the archaeological ruins at Babylon, for instance, is a five-thousand-year-old "Procession Street," which led to a temple. Processions may be somber or festive, triumphant or devout. They usually involve priests, altar servers and often other liturgical ministers. At times, a few of the laity will represent the congregation; on other occasions, the entire congregation takes part.

In addition to the various processions that take place during the Mass, liturgical processions also mark special feast days. These may take place within the church or outside. For example, on Passion (Palm) Sunday, the faithful might gather outdoors for the blessing of palms, then process into the church with their palms. Later in Holy Week, on Holy Thursday, the Blessed Sacrament is taken in silent procession by celebrant and servers to the altar of repose. On Good Friday, the congregation processes to the sanctuary to venerate a large wooden cross. Stations of the Cross, involving a procession from one station to the next, is a ritual pilgrimage.

Other festive occasions include the Candlemas Day procession, when candles are lit, blessed and carried by the assembly as part of that feast day's observance. For the early summer Feast of the Body and Blood of Christ, the Blessed Sacrament, in the monstrance, may be carried through the streets of the neighborhood (if local circumstances permit the ritual to be conducted with dignity), or it could be done within church grounds, or in the building itself. In the past, highly elaborate "Corpus Christi" processions often eclipsed the feast day Mass itself.

Devotional processions were also common in the past and are still popular in other cultures. Many centered around devotions in honor of Mary. Most parishes held a May Day celebration in which her statue was carried aloft, accompanied by clergy and a multitude of altar servers. The First Communion class, girls in white dresses and veils, boys in white shirts and dark trousers, also had a role in the procession. The high point was a crowning of Mary's statue with a wreath of flowers. Processions might also be held in honor of various saints dear to the parish community.

Pilgrimage

For Christians, the tradition of pilgrimage began shortly after Jesus' death and Resurrection, as a way of commemorating the sites associated with those events. A pilgrimage to a sacred place can be done simply as an act of devotion. But people also undertake such journeys in petition (to a shrine noted for miracle cures, for instance) or in thanksgiving for a favor granted. In medieval times, pilgrimages were often assigned as penance for sin.

During the Middle Ages, despite the rigors of travel, pilgrimage to the Holy Land reached its greatest popularity. Today the most important places of pilgrimage are the Holy Land, Rome, the Marian shrines and Assisi, home of Francis and Clare.

When people go on pilgrimage, it is customary to bring back holy water from a healing shrine, or a vial of water from a sacred river (like the Jordan) or sea (Galilee) or perhaps a bit of soil or a few stones from land regarded as holy.

Other Ways of Being Catholic

Catholics find that even the simplest acts enrich their faith, for example, the custom of bowing the head out of reverence when saying or hearing the name of Jesus or making the Sign of the Cross when an emergency vehicle passes. In times past, a "good" Catholic would not dream of walking by a church without at least a brief visit to the Blessed Sacrament. The high incidence of urban crime, unfortunately, prompts most city churches to lock their doors once services are over.

The symbolism behind some practices gets lost in time. One such is the wearing of new clothes at Easter. Originally this stemmed from newly baptized adults in the early Church putting on white garments to symbolize their new life in the Church. Our "Easter Parade" takes on spiritual meaning when we realize this.

For Further Reading

Kenny, John J. *Now That You Are a Catholic: An Informal Guide to Catholic Customs, Traditions and Practices.* Mahwah, N.J.: Paulist Press, 1986.

CHAPTER ELEVEN

Ethnic Customs

The Catholic Church is universal but not uniform. This is especially true in the American Catholic Church, which is more pluralistic in membership today than ever before. Ours is also an age when ethnic heritage is highly treasured, and the preservation of a culture's religious customs make up an important part of that heritage. To better understand the feelings of ethnic groups presently working to maintain their identity, we need only take a short look back.

With the arrival of great waves of Catholic immigrants from Europe in the nineteenth and early twentieth centuries, "national" parishes were established: Italian, Polish, German, Irish, for example. They were ministered to by priests who spoke their language, and who probably were immigrants themselves. This was especially the case in large cities, where ethnic groups tended to settle in their own identifiable neighborhoods. Otherwise, people willingly traveled across town to hear preaching in their own language and to enjoy the fellowship of others who shared their culture. In mixed parishes, priests might be brought in to hear confessions in the native tongue of whatever nationalities were in sizable numbers in the parish. It took generations before Catholics with European roots could be assimilated into the mainstream of American culture (for many, not until after World War II).

The late twentieth century is witnessing new waves of Catholic immigrants, this time from Latin American and Asian countries. Add to these groups the African-American and Native-American Catholics whose historical circumstances make theirs a culture apart too. All groups look for a sense of belonging in their faith community: a place of both social and spiritual refuge, where religious customs can be preserved.

Some of these someday may be woven into the fabric of American Catholicism, just as happened with many customs of European nations which have become so much a part of the common culture that they are now simply "Catholic."

Customs of European Origin

Among the religious customs that originated in various European nations, the best known are those related to the major seasons in the Church year: Advent-Christmas and Lent-Easter. An immigrant group might bring to America a beloved custom which proved appealing to a wider audience, was copied by others and became part of the common Catholic heritage.

The Christmas tree, along with the Nativity scene and the Advent wreath, were all home customs that worked their way into the worship environment despite their never being part of the official liturgy. In many churches, before Mass begins on the First Sunday of Advent, we see the blessing of the Advent wreath in the sanctuary, with the lighting of an additional candle on the next three Sundays. Much of what takes place in the Christmas Season started in Germany. The Advent wreath, by the way, was a sixteenth-century Lutheran idea, happily borrowed by German Catholics.

The Advent Calendar also has German origins. Intended for children, the calendar may be merry or religious in design. Each day the child opens a "window" of the calendar, according to numbered days. It reveals a scene or symbol or sometimes a verse pointing toward the feast. The last to be opened is the "door" to a Nativity scene.

While evidence shows that from the first centuries the Bethlehem crib appeared in church services, the Christmas manger scene in its present form was popularized by St. Francis of Assisi (who included live animals in an outdoor setting). From Italy, the custom eventually spread throughout the world. Nothing at Christmas is more "Catholic" than this portrayal of the Nativity.

The Christmas tree evolved from the medieval Paradise Tree hung with apples, used to depict the story of Adam and

Eve's fall from grace. This was part of the Advent plays once presented in European churches. (When the performances got too rowdy, they were no longer allowed in church.) The tree was so loved by the people, they began setting them up at home (again, the Germans get credit), and adding symbols. The evergreen itself signifies eternity, and the lights represent Christ as the light of the world. Other ornaments include angels and the star of Bethlehem. Though not liturgical, the Christmas tree too has found its way into the sanctuary of just about every church.

The Irish custom of putting a light in the window to welcome Christ was used to let priests—who had been outlawed by the British at the time of the English occupation of Ireland—know that this house welcomed them.

Outside of Church, Easter generally has never been celebrated in the United States to the degree of Christmas festivities. But there is the pre-Lenten celebration of Mardi Gras (literally, "fat Tuesday"). (The pan-European custom of carnival has other names as well, according to the country.) Because medieval penitential regulations were so rigorous, carnival offered the last chance for reveling in rich foods, as well as clearing these foods away before the beginning of Lent. Pageants, balls and other high-spirited activities were also part of the festivities.

Easter ethnic customs are marked by symbolic foods. At one time, eggs were a forbidden food during Lent. Their appearance at the Easter table, therefore, was most welcome. Dyed in bright colors as a sign of rejoicing, the eggs were further decorated with intricate designs in some Eastern European countries—developing it into an art form. In religious symbolism, the unbroken egg is like the rock tomb of Christ; broken, it is a sign of Christ and new life emerging at the Resurrection.

Another traditional food, the hot cross bun, is believed to have originated in a fourteenth-century English monastery. Monks would distribute buns with icing in the design of a cross to the poor on Good Friday. Eventually this became a specialty for all of Lent.

European immigrants, particularly from France and

Germany, also brought with them the observance of Name Day. Comparable to a birthday, this is celebrated on the feast day of the saint for whom a person is named and includes feasting with family and friends as well as gifts.

Hispanic-American Customs

In the changing composition of the American Church, the Hispanic population is showing the most growth—representing between twenty-five and thirty percent of all American Catholics at present. Anywhere from two to four million undocumented aliens may also figure into this number. The greatest proportion of Hispanics are of Mexican heritage, but there are also significant numbers of Puerto Ricans and Cubans as well as political and economic refugees from Central and South American countries.

The richness of religious traditions in Hispanic culture is evident in the abundance of customs related not just to feasts of the Church year, but also in special devotions and practices surrounding home and family.

On the festive list is the nine-day *Las Posadas*—"inn" or "lodgings"—beginning December 16. (The nine symbolizes the nine months Mary carried Jesus in her womb.) This pre-Christmas pageant re-enacts the Holy Family's search for shelter. Each evening, two people chosen to represent Joseph and Mary proceed from house to house (three or four, pre-selected), but are turned away. Other parishioners accompany the couple with lighted candles until, at last, an "innkeeper" invites them in, treating everyone to hot chocolate and pastries. The final night, Christmas Eve, ends on church grounds. Here—or sometimes in a nearby home—the children break a piñata filled with candy and other treats. The doors to the church (the "inn") are opened, and the group processes in, singing and praying. (Breaking a piñata began as a teaching tool by Franciscans in Mexico. The piñata represented the devil and it was struck with the "rod of virtue.")

Another pre-Christmas observance is the *Novena de Aguinaldo*, consisting of daily morning Mass for nine days.

Attendance at Mass is seen as a gift (*aguinaldo*) to the Child Jesus.

On one of the most heavily attended liturgies of the year, Ash Wednesday, Hispanics acknowledge that despite their sinfulness, they belong to Christ. On Palm Sunday, the palms they receive are either placed on the *altarcito*, the little altar at home, or on doors or windows as a symbol of protection.

The feast of St. John the Baptist, on June 24, is popular among Hispanics everywhere, but especially so for Puerto Ricans, as St. John is patron of the capital city of their native country (San Juan). The day appropriately begins at the beach—water, of course, being associated with the Baptist. Throughout the day, people "baptize" each other on the street. Anyone traversing a neighborhood where this custom is kept alive should remember to wear old or waterproof clothes.

Another festive day, despite the mournful-sounding name, is *El Día de los Muertos* (the Day of the Dead) on November 2—the Hispanic equivalent of All Souls' Day. All traditions are a way of linking the past with the present. This one, in addition, links two worlds: earth and eternity. At the feast day Mass, loaves of a special sweet bread baked in the shape of human figures are presented along with the gifts of bread and wine, then blessed and distributed at the end of Mass. Families gather at the cemetery, where they clean and decorate the graves of their deceased members. Here too they enjoy a graveside picnic lunch, for theirs is the Christian attitude toward death: one of hope and new life.

Under the title of Our Lady of Guadalupe, Mary, as the patron of Mexico, receives particular veneration by Mexican-Americans on her feast, December 12. They recall the story of how the Virgin appeared to Juan Diego, a peasant, on the outskirts of Mexico City on December 12, 1531. She left an imprint of her dark-skinned image on his cloak, which is now enshrined in the cathedral built on the site. Guadalupe is probably the greatest place of pilgrimage in the Americas. (The twelfth day of each month is also one of special homage to Our Lady.)

In customs centering around the family, there is the practice, for instance, of naming a baby after the saint on whose feast day the baby was born. The godparents at Baptism not only have an important role then; they become *compadres* of the parents—close friends based on a spiritual relationship— which creates a special bond between them that is intended to last a lifetime.

When a daughter reaches the age of fifteen, the celebration called a *quinceañera*, "fifteen years," sometimes equals a wedding in lavishness. Along with marking her social maturity, it can also signify her readiness for Christian commitment.

At the day's Mass, the girl takes part in ceremonies that include leaving her rosary, prayer book and a bouquet of flowers at Mary's altar. (Flowers have long been a sacramental symbol for Hispanics—representing new life arising from the earth.) During the Presentation of Gifts, the girl receives a crown, holy medal and ring, and renews her baptismal promises. The celebration concludes that evening with a dinner, reception and formal ball.

Blessings are given on many occasions, and not only by a priest. Parents often bless their children with the Sign of the Cross before putting them to bed. Family and friends bless each other in traditional forms. For example, someone who is leaving on a journey will be wished a *"Vaya con Díos"* ("May God accompany you").

Hispanics show gratitude to God in expressive ways. In petitionary prayer, in the case of illness, a *promesa* ("promise") may be made to God; if the prayer is answered with a cure, the promise must be fulfilled. It might be having a Mass said in thanksgiving, or making an offering at the altar of a particular church or shrine. A common offering is a *milagrito*, a small charm, often of silver or gold, in the shape of the body part that has been cured. Sometimes the altar is approached by the person's "walking" the length of the church on one's knees (*de rodillas*).

Asian-American Customs

The newest wave of immigrants brings Catholics from a number of Asian countries, including political refugees from

Kampuchea (Cambodia), Laos and Vietnam. The subject of religious traditions of Asian origin is one of vastness and diversity. Here we must limit ourselves to a few examples chosen from the Philippines, the only Catholic country in Asia (more than eighty percent of the population), and from South Korea, which has the fastest-growing Catholic population among Asians (150,000 to 200,000 converts each year in that country).

Processions, novenas and special devotions mark the spirituality of Filipino-Americans. Many traditions show the influence of Spain, colonial ruler of the Philippines for almost four hundred years—but always with a Filipino flavor. The week- and even month-long religious festivals of the Philippines, when transferred to the United States, are often capsulized into a single grand liturgy. An example of this is *Santacruzan*, a May flower festival replete with pageantry. It commemorates the fourth-century search for the True Cross in the Holy Land by Queen Helena, mother of the Roman Emperor Constantine. When celebrated as a Sunday liturgy, Santacruzan begins with an impressive procession that includes persons representing characters from both the Old and New Testaments. Others symbolize faith, hope, charity, justice and wisdom. There will be angels and Roman soldiers, flower girls and their escorts, and one young woman selected for the role of Queen Helena, while a young man acts as Constantine. Santacruzan is a splendid mix of religious history and legend in which, in the end, Queen Helena discovers the cross and brings it in triumph to Rome.

Two feasts eliciting the deepest love and greatest devotion concern Christ. The first, on January 9, centers on the Black Nazarene, represented by a statue depicting Christ carrying the Cross. The original, carved in black wood by Mexican Indians, was transported to the Philippines by the Spanish, and is enshrined in a Manila church. This Black Christ is honored with a perpetual novena. Any time a replica of the highly prized statue can be obtained by a community of Filipino-Americans, it can occasion both a Mass of celebration and a novena. Families may take turns keeping the statue, a week at a time, in their home, where Friday devotions are held.

101

The other feast, on the third weekend of January, honors *Santo Niño*, the Holy Child. Here too the cult of devotion surrounds a statue of religious and historical significance. The original foot-high image of the Christ Child was a baptismal gift of Magellan in 1521 to a converted chieftain and his queen. The statue resides in a church in Cebu City, oldest city in the Philippines. The highlight of a Sunday liturgy for this feast is the traditional blessing given to the Christ Child images that Filipino-Americans bring to Mass.

Christmas for them is an especially festive season. During the nine days preceding the feast, they may observe either or both of the following: a novena of Masses called *misa de gallo* (cock-crow Masses, referring to the early hour), and a pageant similar to the Hispanic Las Posadas, but called in the native Tagalog language *Panuluvan*. When a family hangs a *parol*, or star-shaped lantern in the window, it means the Holy Family will find welcome, and therefore all are welcome (a sign of Filipino hospitality).

Two of the important festivals that Korean-Americans observe are days which include honoring the dead. In determining these feasts, they use the lunar calendar, so dates vary from one year to the next. One feast comes at the start of the lunar year, somewhere around February (their New Year's Day, in effect). The other, the Autumn Evening Festival, is celebrated somewhat like an American Thanksgiving. Certain foods are eaten, such as a special kind of rice cake. It is a commemoration of family and of personal history— remembering and honoring ancestors. On both feasts, food is traditionally taken to the graveside of deceased family members. And of course there is a feast-day Mass.

Korean communities don't forget their martyrs either. Though Christianity came late to Korea, only two hundred years ago, in the number of canonized saints, the country ranks fourth after Italy, Spain and France. During the nineteenth century, thousands of Korean Catholics died in three great waves of persecution. Recognizing their sacrifice, Pope John Paul II in 1984 canonized one hundred three martyrs in a single ceremony (ninety-three were Korean while the other ten were French missionaries). Their feast day on September 20 is a memorial for Andrew Kim Taegon (first Korean priest), Paul Chong Hasang (lay apostle) and martyred companions.

Korean-Americans continue to be eager witnesses of their faith, evangelizing many converts from among the other, newer immigrants from their homeland. One tool of evangelization grows out of their involvement in the Legion of Mary, which was introduced into Korea by an Irish missionary. Korean culture admires a strong organizational structure with attendant leadership characteristics of the Legion. There was the added appeal that the laity could head the organization, women playing a role too. While they tend to be well-educated, women were ordinarily housebound, with little outlet for their skills. Catholic husbands made the exception of allowing their wives to go to meetings of the Legion since it was to help the Church. The Legion's requirement of a minimum two hours' weekly for visitations to the sick and needy gave women their opportunity.

Faith-sharing in small groups is another practice Korean Catholics have brought with them. Typically, various groups of parishioners will meet twice a month in their homes, using Scripture readings as the basis for their discussions. (Catholic leadership in Korea borrowed the structure of the small group meeting from a government program aimed at propagandizing, then turned the concept toward a spiritual goal.)

African-American Customs

While European immigrants of the past attended their "national" parishes out of choice, Catholics of African-American heritage were more often obliged to go to the "black" church, whether it was in their own neighborhood or on the other side of town. Their local parish may have scheduled Masses for black parishioners at a time different from whites, or seated them separately in back pews or the galleries. Even today many African-Americans prefer going to the black church in town, wherever it is located, because it is the place where they feel most at home both spiritually and socially.

Moreover, because there were (and are) so few black priests and bishops to speak on their behalf, the laity assumed leadership roles and active involvement long before Vatican II directives for the universal Church encouraged it. Nowhere is this lay participation in their faith community more evident than at Mass.

Catholics experiencing an African-American liturgy for the first time will immediately notice the gospel music. With blues and jazz incorporated into the music, it can be either jubilant or soulful. Accompanying instruments typically include piano, saxophone, cymbals and drums. Both choir and assembly move with the music, swaying, waving their arms above their heads, and clapping their hands. Prayer is an expression of body and soul.

The preaching on the word follows black tradition, which stresses dialogue, not monologue. A spirit-filled Baptist influence in African-American culture as a whole carries over to a preaching style strong on interaction. For example, the preacher interlaces the sermon with questions, to which people affirm their vigorous "Amens" or other responses. As the sermon builds to a climax, a chant-like refrain often punctuates it.

Black Catholics get so caught up in the liturgy that Mass can easily run from an hour and a half to two hours. At the Sign of Peace, for instance, it is not uncommon for greetings to be exchanged for upwards of ten minutes as the assembly acknowledges the presence of Christ in each other. The recessional hymn may extend for an additional ten minutes after the celebrant and servers have exited.

In the worship environment, efforts have begun to offer black saints as role models. The seventeenth-century St. Martin de Porres ranks high on the list. Peruvian-born of a Spanish father and black mother, he became a Dominican brother and friend of the poor. The object of so much discrimination himself, he made it his mission in life to be a reconciler and healer in race relations.

No African-American saint has been canonized yet, though the diocesan process has started for two candidates who lived in the nineteenth century: Mother Mary Elizabeth Lange, founder of the first order for black sisters in the United States, and Pierre Toussaint, an ex-slave and layman renowned for his charitable works. Both emigrated to this country: She from Cuba and he from Haiti.

Outside of the liturgy, networking is a characteristic in African-American parishes. For example, when a member dies, the word spreads quickly, and the women get together to arrange a reception after the funeral or whatever else needs doing. No one has to be asked.

The Knights of Peter Claver, aided by a Ladies Auxiliary, make up an important service group in black Catholic communities. The Knights got their start in 1909, during an era when blacks were refused admittance into the Knights of Columbus. (St. Peter Claver was a seventeenth-century Spanish Jesuit who devoted his life to caring for the needs of slaves in the New World.)

Native American Customs

A sense of the sacred in the whole of creation permeates Native American spirituality. Religious traditions pre-date the arrival of missionaries in the New World in the sixteenth century. In the various tribal languages, the name for God might be the Great Spirit, Creator, Mystery—the idea being that God is beyond human understanding. Whatever the name, the original inhabitants of the land believed in one Supreme Being. Until very recent times, missionaries attempted to stamp out the religious customs and ceremonies of Indians, viewing them as "pagan." (Jesuits are among those in the Church now making a concerted effort to rectify a wrong.)

Native American Catholics (twenty percent of the total Native American population) today find that they can practice their Catholic faith without abandoning their identity as a people. Because religion was never compartmentalized, it has remained an integral part of the culture.

Though some four hundred fifty tribes are found in North America, each with customs and traditions of their own, nevertheless, general observations as well as specific examples can show how native spirituality exists side-by-side with Catholicism.

Anticipating environmentalists by many centuries, their creation-centered spirituality looks for a harmonious relationship with God, creation and each other. This interdependency is symbolized by the sacred circle, part of many rituals and religious thought itself. Elements of the earth—for example, water, sage and sweet grass—are also basic to ceremonies. In recognition of the gifts of nature, ritual dances are given names such as corn, eagle, buffalo and sun. Dance and song have always been important to native worship. The drum is one of the main instruments. Drumming signifies the heartbeat of creation.

Rich in sacramentals and symbolism, native ceremonies are sometimes incorporated into the liturgy, as happens at the annual Native American Mass in Santa Fe's cathedral. The Penitential Rite has been done in the form of a cleansing ceremony typical of many tribes in the Southwest. The water is blessed by tribal elders, and each person is invited to drink the water, asking God to cleanse them of sins. During the offering of gifts, the incensing ingredients may come from blessed, burned evergreen, representing everlasting life. In a naming and blessing ritual, tribal elders give honor to the celebrant at the Mass with a blessing and a Native American name. A naming expresses and establishes a close relationship between the recipient and the tribe.

The Southwest is home to some of the largest concentrations of Native American Catholics. In most of their pueblos (independent villages) they hold an annual feast-day celebration to pay homage to the patron saint of each village church.

Ascetic practices are a traditional means of seeking a higher level of spirituality. Fasting, for example, from food and water while in the wilderness for four days is part of the "vision quest" of a young man. The Plains Indian women belonging to a guild that does quillwork must fast and pray before commencing the work.

Asceticism marked the life of the seventeenth century Mohawk, Blessed Kateri Tekakwitha, beatified in 1980—the first Native American to be considered for sainthood. The Tekakwitha Conference in Great Falls, Montana, named in her honor, serves as organizational headquarters for Native American Catholics. Through the conference, the different tribes come together to share their faith and reinforce it.

For Further Reading

Brown, Joseph Epes. *The Spiritual Legacy of the American Indian.* New York: The Crossroad Publishing Company, 1986.

Davis, Cyprian, O.S.B. *The History of Black Catholics in the United States.* New York: The Crossroad Publishing Company, 1990.

Department of Education, United States Catholic Conference. *Faith and Culture: A Multicultural Catechetical Resource.* Washington, D.C.: USCC, 1987.

Elizondo, Rev. Virgilio. *Christianity and Culture.* Huntington, Ind.: Our Sunday Visitor, 1975.

Mexican-American Cultural Center. *Faith Expressions of Hispanics in the Southwest.* San Antonio, Texas, 1990.

CHAPTER TWELVE

How the Church Is Run

The Vatican

The Vatican (from the Latin for "hill") is a sovereign state with a resident population of about one thousand. It has its own diplomatic corps, civil service, post office, banking system and even a jail. Some nine hundred million Roman Catholics around the globe (twenty percent of the world's population) look to the Vatican as the center of their religion.

Located on the west bank of the Tiber River, this independent state covers 108.7 acres and is entirely surrounded by the city of Rome. Some church properties are located in Rome itself, and the Vatican has extraterritorial rights to this land. Rights extend also to the summer papal residence at Castel Gandolfo, seventeen miles southeast of Rome.

Pilgrims on a visit to the Vatican are drawn first to the Basilica of St. Peter's, largest church in the world, built over the site of the Apostle Peter's tomb. Other attractions include the Vatican museums, galleries and library, which contain unsurpassed treasures, rare books and manuscripts. But most of all, visiting Catholics hope for a glimpse of the pope. Unless he is on a papal trip or at his summer residence, the pope gives a general audience every Wednesday. Depending upon the weather, this takes place either in St. Peter's Square or in the nearby General Audience Hall. In the summer, he gives a regular audience at Castel Gandolfo. In addition, each Sunday at noon, from his apartments above the square, the pope gives a general blessing to the thousands who gather there. A ticket obtained in advance is required for the general audience, but not for the Sunday blessing.

Holding ceremonies and welcoming visitors are only a small part of the work that goes on daily at the Vatican. This central headquarters of Roman Catholicism is often referred to as the "Holy See." The term *see*, derived from the Latin *sedes*, or chair, signifying the episcopal chair or throne reserved in every cathedral for its bishop, denotes a bishop's authority. In this case, the authority of the bishop of Rome is worldwide.

While St. Peter's immense size and splendor make it the logical setting for canonizations and other large-scale ceremonies, the cathedral for the Bishop of Rome (the pope) is St. John Lateran, the first basilica in Rome, dedicated in 324. (The anniversary of its dedication, November 9, is a universal feast day.) Until the fourteenth century, the Pope lived next door to the cathedral, in the Lateran Palace, a gift from the Emperor Constantine. The basilica is named for St. John the Baptist. The inscription above its entry proclaims: "Mother and Head of all Churches in the City and throughout the World."

The parish church for residents of the Vatican is St. Ann, located near St. Ann's Gate, the employees' entrance, which lies north of St. Peter's Square. The North American church in Rome—Santa Susanna—is an excellent source of information about things Catholic for American pilgrims. English is spoken there.

The Pope

As head of the Church, the pope holds supreme authority. This authority—executive, legislative and judicial—is generally exercised through the various agencies of the Vatican, but the pope is free to act alone or with members of the hierarchy advising him. The pope pronounces on official Church teaching, presides at major gatherings and ceremonies, and appoints new cardinals, archbishops and bishops. As administrator, teacher, moral leader and symbol of Church unity, he sets the tone for the Church. The more charismatic and active the pontiff is, the greater moral influence he wields among both Church members and the wider world.

One avenue for teaching is the encyclical letter, a writing which the pope may address to his bishops, or to the faithful at large, on important matters ranging from Christian marriage and family to statements on peace and social justice.

In 1870, infallibility became Church doctrine. This means that the Church, guided by the Spirit, cannot make a fundamental error in matters of faith and morals. The pope and the college of bishops are infallible when solemnly teaching a revealed truth. Only one doctrine—the Assumption of Mary into Heaven, declared to be true in 1950—has been declared as infallible.

Sacred College of Cardinals

Assisting the pope as advisers and administrators are the cardinals, now numbering more than one hundred sixty. Their most visible role comes at the death of a pope, when they must elect a new one. This gathering of cardinals, called a consistory, takes place in the historic Sistine Chapel, where votes must be cast for candidates from among their own members until a successor is elected.

On a regular basis, some cardinals are assigned full time at the Vatican. The majority, however, continue to reside in and govern their own episcopal see. (Cardinals tend to be archbishops in the larger archdioceses.) Though the added title does not increase a man's sacramental powers, a cardinal will have greater jurisdictional power as well as greater influence. A cardinal's duties may be expanded to include service on the board of directors for different Vatican agencies, which entails periodic travel to Rome. After age eighty, a cardinal is no longer eligible to vote in papal elections, but he does remain a member of the Sacred College.

The college as an institution dates to the twelfth century. Before then, the Bishop of Rome used as his advisers clergy from the principal churches of Rome. For many centuries, most cardinals were Italian, as was the pope. Increasingly today, though the largest number come from European countries, there is growing representation from other continents, making the college more reflective of world Catholicism.

The Roman Curia are the administrative units that conduct the business of the universal Church: the Secretariat of State, congregations, tribunals, councils and offices. The general arrangement goes back to the sixteenth century. While laypersons work in the various agencies, many of the employees are priests or religious.

The congregations deal with matters such as liturgical changes, missionary work, the clergy, religious orders, canonization proceedings and coordination of international relief services. Cardinals serve as the chief executive officers of these congregations; they are akin to cabinet-level ministers. The most influential of these is the cardinal heading the Congregation of the Doctrine of the Faith, which is concerned with maintaining orthodoxy. But the most powerful position, second only to the pope, is the secretary of state, who deals with all curial departments and otherwise acts as the pope's right-hand man.

The tribunals, or judicial agencies, deal with matters such as marriage questions that have been appealed from the local level. The Church legal system is based on canon law: a body of rules covering all facets of ecclesiastical government. The first general codification occurred in 1917, and a revised code of 1,752 canons was issued in 1983. The Code of Canon Law, published in English translation, is available in some libraries.

Among the other curial agencies, the twelve councils and three offices take care of an assortment of matters, from those considered by the Council for Interreligious Dialogue to issues related to Vatican employees which come before a Labor Office.

Every five years, diocesan bishops are required to go to Rome for an *ad limina* (Latin for "to the threshold") visit. This is symbolic of a pilgrim visit to the tombs of Sts. Peter and Paul. Before meeting with the pope and Vatican officials, each bishop must provide a detailed report on conditions in his diocese. The practice began in the last half of the nineteenth century, during the reign of Pius IX. The approximately four hundred American prelates usually make their visits in regional groupings on a staggered schedule.

Vatican Diplomatic Corps

Through the department of the Secretariat of State, the pope sends representatives to more than one hundred countries. The Vatican also has permanent observer status at the United Nations. In addition to their ambassadorial duties— maintaining contact between a country's dioceses and the Vatican—papal representatives play an important consultative role in naming new bishops for the country to which they are assigned.

There are different grades of representation. A nuncio (from the Latin for "messenger") is equivalent to full ambassadorial rank. Because the Vatican's diplomatic corps has long been highly regarded around the world, a papal nuncio is traditionally viewed as dean of the foreign diplomatic circle on occasions of ceremonies.

A pro-nuncio has accreditation as an ambassador, but does not qualify for the honor of dean of diplomats. The United States has had a pro-nuncio since 1984, when full diplomatic relations with the Vatican were restored. A ban on relations with the Holy See had been enacted by Congress in 1867, due to anti-Catholic feeling. In 1939 President Franklin Roosevelt appointed a personal envoy to the pope and that arrangement continued until 1984.

The American Church

The Catholic Church in the United States operates at various levels: national, state, regional, (arch)diocesan and local parish.

At the national level, the National Conference of Catholic Bishops (NCCB), including all bishops, archbishops and cardinals, is the public voice for the Church in this country. The United States Catholic Conference (USCC) serves as the bishops' operational agency. Both the NCCB and the USCC have their headquarters in Washington, D.C.

The bishops elect a president and other officers for three-year terms to represent them at national and international meetings. With Vatican approval, the conference sets national policy for the Church. At the annual general meeting, a two-thirds' vote of the membership is required to pass resolutions and issues. Though probably best known for the pastoral letters on peace and the economy issued in recent years, the organization deals primarily with concerns such as the liturgy, vocations and doctrinal matters. The bishops make decisions based on input from about two dozen working committees. The programs that result are then carried out by the staff at the U.S. Catholic Conference.

Bishops' conferences in various nations are a relatively new development. In most cases, they began after Vatican II. In the American Church, however, the pattern was set earlier, with the establishment of a national council in 1917 to deal with war relief. It was known as the National Catholic War Council. International welfare remains a concern of the NCCB; its aid is administered by Catholic Relief Services. In 1919 it became the National Catholic Welfare Conference. The NCCB in its present form dates from 1966. It has served as a model for national conferences set up in other countries.

On a more modest scale, state conferences also develop programs and otherwise make the voice of the Church heard on matters of public concern for their area. Representatives to a state conference may include both clergy and laity, who are delegated by their dioceses to carry out the work at that level.

The American Church is divided into thirty-three regional ecclesiastical provinces, each geographical area being comprised of an archdiocese headed by an archbishop along with one or more dioceses, each headed by a bishop. For example, the Province of Seattle includes the Archdiocese of Seattle, the Diocese of Spokane and the Diocese of Yakima. Bishops of a province have a role (though not a decisive one) in the selection process for new bishops in their region. They meet to discuss possible candidates; after a secret vote, the names are forwarded to the pro-nuncio in Washington, D.C., who sends the names and an evaluation to Rome.

The archbishop is the "metropolitan" for the province, as his is the chief diocese for the region. His actual jurisdiction over the smaller dioceses is limited, though he enjoys more prestige and influence than a bishop. Each bishop has ultimate responsibility for the administration of his diocese.

An archbishop may have an auxiliary bishop to help him with administration. If the Vatican designates this assistant to be next in line of succession, he is ranked as a coadjutor bishop. In the other dioceses of the province, an assistant bishop is technically called a suffragan. A bishop is sometimes referred to as the "ordinary" (in the sense of being an overseer).

Other aides in an archdiocese or diocese could include a vicar general, chancellor, vice-chancellor and department heads for Catholic schools, community services and so on. The central office is commonly called the "chancery." The larger an archdiocese, the more numerous are divisions and subdivisions of government.

In addition to acting as chief administrator, the bishop holds in trust the Church property of his diocese. Through writings and speeches, the bishop maintains the Church's teachings on faith and morals, which is one of his paramount obligations. He is also expected to conduct a schedule of visitations to every parish in his diocese.

A major concern for every bishop is the welfare of his priests. A diocesan priest, that is, one not connected with a particular religious order, receives his seminary training under the auspices of the diocese in which he plans to serve. Once ordained, he is under a promise of obedience to his bishop, who assigns him to parish work or other responsibilities.

Within a diocese, clusters of neighboring parishes are grouped into subdivisions called deaneries (or vicariates). Led by a priest of one of the parishes (called dean, or vicar forane), the deanery meets regularly to promote common pastoral action for the area. The dean sees that the clergy in his deanery fulfill their obligations as well as get help with problems. A diocese may also have a priests' council or senate with input on matters in the diocese.

The bishop must appoint a censor to review material in Catholic books and pamphlets before they reach print, to be sure writings on doctrinal matters are in accord with Church teaching. When a work is approved, the censor gives a *Nihil Obstat* ("Nothing Stands in the Way"), which permits the bishop to grant his *Imprimatur* ("Let It Be Printed"). This approval does not necessarily imply agreement with a publication's content or opinions. Catholic publishers note the censor's approval on the copyright page of the book or pamphlet.

Religious Communities

Religious communities are variously known by names such as order, congregation, society or institute of consecrated life. The comprehensive technical term is "religious institute," although almost everyone tends to say "order." Priests belonging to such communities are known as "Regular" clergy because they observe the rule (*regula* in Latin) of the religious community they join.

Each of these orders has its own constitution and rule of life by which its members live. The rule must receive Vatican approval. Religious communities may be clerical—that is, composed solely of priests, or a combination of clerics and lay brothers (men not ordained but taking vows), or of religious women (sisters or nuns). An order might be international in scope (for example, the Jesuits), limited to an apostolate within one country (for example, in the United States, the Sisters of the Blessed Sacrament for Indians and Colored People, founded by Blessed Katharine Drexel).

When an order extends over a wide geographical area, it is divided into provinces, each headed by a provincial. All of the order's religious houses within a given area belong to that province, much as all the parishes in a specified territory belong to one diocese. At the local level, some communities elect their own superiors. In other cases, superiors might be appointed by the overall head of the order. Generally, a provincial, national or international head is elected according to the order's constitution. Heads of religious communities are known by a variety of titles such as superior general, mother superior, abbot, abbess, prior, prioress.

While many orders have a form of centralized government, with a chain of command reaching down to the local level, monastic institutes tend to operate autonomously, with each house (monastery, abbey or priory) governing itself but linked to a federation of the independent houses in order to provide mutual support in addition to setting and maintaining standards. All orders come under the scrutiny and authority of the designated congregations that form part of the Roman Curia.

Members of a religious community owe their allegiance to that community. Priests assigned to ministry in a diocese will come under the authority of the bishop as well as the community's superior. If conflicts arise, differences must be worked out between bishop and superior.

International and national conferences of superiors promote effective ministry, cooperation and understanding among the different religious institutes. The United States, for instance, has a Leadership Conference of Women Religious and a Conference of Major Superiors of Men.

How to Address Clergy and Others in Religious Life

When speaking to a priest, the general rule is to address him as "Father (last name)." Some religious orders, such as the Franciscans, prefer a "Father (first name)." When in doubt, a simple "Father" will do.

If a priest has the additional title of Monsignor, call him "Monsignor (last name)." Monsignor (literally, "my lord") is an honorary title granted by the pope and confers no jurisdictional power in itself. Older priests may receive this title as a reward for accomplishments. Younger priests may be singled out as monsignors if they are in line for higher ecclesial office.

For those in religious life, you usually say "Sister (first name)," or "Brother (first name)." Again, simply using the title will do.

When speaking to a deacon, "Mr. (last name)" is correct.

For a cardinal, archbishop or bishop, title and last name is proper. In the past, "Your Excellency" was used for bishops and archbishops, and "Your Eminence" for cardinals, but Americans are no longer inclined toward these terms.

Occasionally cardinals may be identified thus: John Cardinal Smith. A seventeenth-century pope thought the honor of being appointed a cardinal was so great that the title should be an integral part of the man's name. This is a fading custom.

The Pope is addressed as "Your Holiness."

In addressing a letter, use the following guidelines:

For a priest—Reverend (full name); if he is a member of a religious order, the initials of the order should follow his name.

For a monsignor—Reverend Monsignor (full name).

Sister or Brother is followed by the full name, with initials of the religious order after it.

For a deacon—Reverend Mr. (full name).

For an archbishop or bishop—The Most Reverend (full name), Archbishop (or Bishop) of the Archdiocese (or Diocese) of....

For a cardinal—His Eminence Cardinal (full name); if he is also the head of an archdiocese, the next line would read, Archbishop of the Archdiocese of....

For the Pope—His Holiness Pope (name). Remember too that the Vatican is not part of Italy. In writing to this destination, make it Vatican City.

For Further Reading

Packard, Jerrold M. *Peter's Kingdom: Inside the Papal City.* New York: Charles Scribner's Sons, 1985.

Reese, Thomas J., S.J. *Archbishop: Inside the Power Structure of the American Catholic Church.* San Francisco: Harper & Row, 1989.

CHAPTER THIRTEEN

The Call to Serve

Every baptized Christian receives a vocation or call to follow Christ and transform the world. In the past, the idea of vocation was limited to ordination or formal vows in religious life. But in the aftermath of Vatican II came a growing awareness that all the faithful—not just Father, Sister or Brother—are called to holiness and service in Christ through a particular state in life. Nevertheless, one of the distinctive marks of the Catholic Church has been a formal commitment to dedicated service to the Church through ordination, religious life or membership in an organized lay apostolate.

The Consecrated Life Today: General Notes

Most religious orders now have a flexible process in which a potential priest, sister or brother can learn more about the community by spending time with its members. A more formal relationship—actually living in community for a period of time—is variously called a candidacy, pre-novitiate or postulancy. The person may continue with the regular business of school or work.

Following this initial period, the next step is the novitiate. The novice shares directly in the work and prayer life of the community during this period of study and spiritual formation. At the end of the novitiate, usually lasting a year or so, a temporary commitment is made through vows or promises for a two- or three-year period in which the person goes on living in the community.

At the end of that time, a final commitment takes place through permanent vows or promises. In the past, an individual may have assumed a new name at the time of ordination or final profession to symbolize the start of a new life, but this is rarely the case now. The usual vows call for poverty, chastity and obedience. Some communities require additional vows. For instance, in a monastic order a vow of stability may be taken, in which the individual promises to remain a part of that community and not move to another house in the order.

Some orders formally present a habit (distinctive apparel) at the time of final profession, in a ceremony called investiture. Others do so at the beginning of the novitiate. Wearing religious dress is both a sign of consecration to God and witness to a life of poverty—that is, detachment from material things. For many orders, wearing a habit is now optional, although some still require it. The orders determine this for themselves, often based on what their ministry or apostolate in the world is.

After final profession, if a sister or brother wishes to be released from vows and re-enter secular life, a request for secularization must be filed with one's religious superior. The request is then sent on for final approval to the Vatican's Congregation for Institutes of Consecrated Life and Societies of Apostolic Life.

The Monastic Life

Monastic life is patterned after the original community of Christians. The Acts of the Apostles tells us: "They devoted themselves to the teaching of the apostles and to the communal life, to the breaking of the bread and to the prayers"; "The community of believers was of one heart and mind, and no one claimed that any of his possessions was his own, but they had everything in common" (Acts 2:42; 4:32).

In the fourth century, when Christianity had become the official religion and increasing numbers joined with varying degrees of belief and commitment, some Christian men and women fled to the desert or countryside to seek an alternative way of living their faith. They began to gather in small communities to share resources and encourage one another's spiritual growth. These groups later developed into monastic communities under ecclesiastical regulation.

A monastic house can vary in size, from several dozen to hundreds of members. A male monastic or monk may be an ordained priest or a brother. Women monastics are called nuns if they are cloistered and dedicated to prayer and meditation; they are known as sisters if they combine the contemplative life with an active ministry.

Monastics attach great importance to prayer, coming together for worship at scheduled times of the day. Prayer and community living give birth to their ministry to others, either within the confines of monastic grounds or away from it.

Each monastic house, in conjunction with its Rule of life, decides what its service will be. Orders with a stricter observance, such as Trappist and Carthusian monks, center prayer and work (intellectual as well as manual) at the home grounds. The Benedictine Rule permits greater freedom of movement, and thus Benedictines are likely to be engaged in apostolates in the wider community.

Although monastics promote a contemplative life-style by remaining separate from the world, they welcome visitors for public prayer times and daily and Sunday Mass. Hospitality has long been a key part of the monastic tradition, and today monastic houses often serve as retreat centers for the laity as well.

The Cloistered Contemplative Life

Alhough monastic houses have varying degrees of enclosure (the extent to which members are free to leave their place of residence for personal business), they are not to be confused with cloistered contemplatives such as the Poor Clares or Discalced Carmelites. The primary ministry of cloistered nuns is prayer; solitude, silence and separation from the world enable them to achieve this purpose. The formation period prior to final profession for this type of life is much longer, averaging from three to nine years.

In a cloistered institute, where members of different

generations, temperaments, social and ethnic backgrounds live closely together, great psychological and spiritual maturity are needed. The rules of enclosure for some orders have been relaxed in recent years, while other orders maintain their traditional seclusion.

Religious Families: Sisters and Brothers

In contrast to monastics and cloistered religious, communities of sisters or brothers dedicate their lives to service in outside ministry. Their apostolate is grounded in prayer and mutual support. Sisters and brothers are "lay" persons, as distinguished from clerics (ordained priests and deacons).

Men can apply to a mixed institute (a community of both priests and brothers) or to an order made up exclusively of brothers. Brother and priest are two distinct vocations; one is not higher or more important than the other. The choice would likely be based on the candidate's talents and the order's particular apostolate.

The Redemptorists, known best for preaching retreats and giving parish missions, and the Franciscans, whose special concern is for the poor, are two examples of mixed institutes. The Brothers of the Christian Schools (Christian Brothers), who focus on education, ranging from teaching in seminaries to running schools for juvenile offenders and serving abroad in missionary schools, is an example of an institute made up exclusively of brothers.

Historically in America and elsewhere, brothers and sisters staffed Catholic schools and hospitals, and some congregations continue in this traditional role. For example, the Alexian Brothers' healing ministry entails hospital chaplaincy and nursing care. On the other hand, while Sisters of the Holy Names of Jesus and Mary still maintain some schools, they more often work in other ministries, such as parish work and direct service to the poor.

For many orders, change came in the aftermath of Vatican II. One of the directives of the Council called for religious communities to reexamine and reflect upon their mission in light of the signs of the times and the purpose of the original founders.

As apostolates expanded to meet the needs of society, particularly among women's congregations, the most visible effects were in dress. Religious habits were updated, for example, a switch to a calf-length skirt instead of one reaching to the shoetops and less restrictive veils, or a switch from the habit to contemporary dress. Sisters no longer had to be accompanied by another member of the community when they went out in public.

Sisters and brothers today work in many new areas of ministry, such as teaching in seminaries or theological unions, administrating diocesan offices and parishes, acting as spiritual directors and giving retreats, counseling families and adult survivors of child sexual abuse, providing prison ministry and campus ministry, operating shelters for the homeless as well as day-care centers, resettling refugees and committing themselves to peace and justice issues.

The Ordained: Priests and Deacons

Diocesan priests in the United States serve primarily in parishes, but they may also work at the chancery, as campus ministers, as chaplains in hospitals or jails, as teachers at the high school or college level, or in other capacities according to the needs of the diocese and their own skills.

Priests belonging to a religious order serve in many of the same capacities as diocesan priests. In the past, many orders had priests to spare and were able to help bishops by staffing some diocesan parishes. But with declining numbers, orders have had to rethink their pastoral assignments. Priority must go to the purpose for which the order was founded, for example, education or missionary work.

Whether a candidate for ordination chooses to be a diocesan priest or one in a religious order, he follows a prescribed course of study beginning with seminary training. Seminaries originated with the sixteenth-century Council of Trent. Prior to that time, candidates for the priesthood received their training in a monastery, at a university, or in a less structured, local "work-study" program under the supervision of a parish priest.

Until recent decades, candidates routinely attended either a diocesan-run seminary or one administered by a religious order. With the decline in priestly vocations, a number of seminaries have been consolidated or closed. As a consequence, students may be sent to an interdiocesan seminary (dioceses pooling their resources), a theological union or a university.

It was once common for a boy to go directly from the eighth grade to a minor seminary (high school level) and, following that, complete his college studies and subsequent training for the priesthood at the major seminary. Today, however, candidates generally have completed college and may even have some work experience behind them before entering serious training for priesthood.

Seminary training today involves a four-year academic course of study along with spiritual formation (growth in the life of prayer). A year of practical experience in ministry under supervision (which can come at any time during a man's candidacy) is also part of the program. Academics cover subjects such as Scripture, Church history, canon law, theology and liturgy. Approximately a year before priestly ordination, the seminarian is ordained as a transitional deacon.

Should a priest wish to return to the lay state, he must file a petition with his bishop (if he is a diocesan priest) or with his religious superior if he belongs to an order. Final approval must come from the Vatican.

Although the majority of Roman Catholic priests are celibate (unmarried), there are some married priests. When a clergyman from another Christian denomination converts to Catholicism, he may apply to be accepted as a priest in the Catholic Church. If he is already married, he may remain so. Celibacy did not become universally mandatory for priests until the twelfth century. Even before this, however, the bishops in some countries required it, and it has been a long-standing tradition in the Roman Church.

Just as religious orders may have distinctive dress, those

who are ordained may wear special clothing, particularly a clerical shirt (traditionally black but now available in other colors as well) with a white band, called a Roman collar. Priests in religious communities may also wear the habit distinctive to their order.

In the past in the United States, and in some countries today, standard clerical garb is the cassock: ankle-length, close-fitting and buttoned down the front. Color varies with rank: white for the pope, red or scarlet for cardinals, purple for bishops and black for priests.

Permanent Deacons

The Acts of the Apostles tells us that the apostles appointed seven men as deacons (from the Greek *diakonia*, meaning service) to care for the material needs of the community (Acts 6:2-6). In a ceremony involving a laying on of hands, the seven were commissioned to distribute alms, freeing the apostles to concentrate on preaching the Good News.

Apostolic times also saw the beginning of the order of widows, whose primary purpose was to visit and pray with the sick. Like the deacons, they lived among the people they served, as members of their local house Church.

In the course of history, permanent deacons (and deaconesses) disappeared from the ecclesiastical scene. Only the transitional diaconate remained as one of the steps toward priesthood. Other minor orders included acolyte and lector, two stages that evolved into today's ministries of altar server and reader.

After Vatican II the permanent diaconate was restored and, in 1968, each diocese in the United States was allowed to develop its own diaconate program according to Church guidelines. At present, about ten thousand permanent deacons are engaged in ministry in the United States.

Deacons visit hospitals, nursing homes and jails, teach Bible study and meet local charitable or educational needs. Many work in parishes as administrators and even pastors. Deacons are qualified to preach, officiate at Baptisms, assist at

125

and bless marriages, lead rites of burial, conduct Communion services and Benediction and take Viaticum to the dying. They cannot hear confessions or consecrate the Eucharist—that is, celebrate the Mass.

To be ordained a deacon, a man must be at least thirty-five. The majority of American deacons are married. If married, his wife must agree to the decision and participate in the program with him. Should his wife die, he is not allowed to remarry. A single candidate promises not to marry after ordination. A promise of obedience to the bishop is part of the ordination ceremony.

The three-year preparation program takes place evenings and weekends, because most candidates work full time in secular jobs and ordinarily continue to do so after ordination. The program generally consists of two years of classes in Scripture, Church history, theology and liturgy, as well as spiritual formation. A third year is given to specialized training.

After ordination, the deacon (and his wife) determines his abilities, looks at the needs of the community, then makes a covenant with the person in charge of the organization involved. For instance, a deacon who wants to do both parish work and ministry to the terminally ill in a hospice would make a covenant with the pastor and the hospice director. Covenants are approved by the bishop.

Secular Institutes

The secular institute is a relatively new type of religious organization. Given full papal approval in 1947, the idea had first surfaced in eighteenth-century Europe. The secular institute differs from the traditional religious community in that its members live the evangelical counsels (poverty, chastity and obedience) in their everyday lives. Their vows or promises are not made publicly, they may or may not live in a community and there is no distinctive dress. Each institute determines the form its organization will take. Members are subject to the diocesan bishop as well as to their own superior.

Institutes come under the ultimate jurisdiction of the Vatican.

Most secular institutes are small. Some have lay members only; others might include diocesan clergy, who are eligible because they do not otherwise belong to a religious community. The aim of members of secular institutes is to seek personal holiness while giving Christian witness in the world.

Missionaries

The United States was itself considered mission territory by the Vatican until 1908. Just three years after that, the first local order of missionaries was established: the Catholic Foreign Mission Society of America, more familiarly known as Maryknoll. Although comprised initially of priests and brothers, a congregation of sisters was founded in 1912 as an outgrowth of laywomen helping the society.

Many other orders have been active in the missionary field. In the sixteenth century the Jesuits began the revolutionary practice of adapting to native cultures rather than imposing Western culture as part of the conversion to Christianity. Conservatives in the Church argued against the method— despite its success—and in 1704 Pope Clement XI put an end to the experiment. Catholic missionaries were banned from countries in the Far East that feared Western imperialism. In recent decades, however, the Jesuits' transcultural approach has become the accepted method of missionary practice.

Missionary work is not confined to members of particular orders. Diocesan clergy as well as priests, brothers and sisters from other religious communities may sign on as volunteers "on loan" from their own bishops or superiors. A five-year commitment is common, allowing time for training in an understanding of the culture and a working knowledge of the native language.

Lay missioners also work in association with missionary agencies. The first formal program, established by Maryknoll, began in 1975. Lay missioners sign a contract, which may be renewable, to serve from three to five years, depending on preparation time required. They work as carpenters, doctors, teachers, mechanics, journalists, farmers, according to individual skills. In addition to the foreign missions, there are home missions such as summer programs in the Appalachians or year-long projects among the urban poor.

Third Orders

Through membership in a secular order—popularly called a third order—Catholic laity bring a religious spirit into the world. St. Francis of Assisi was apparently the first to organize one of these spiritual fraternities. His first order was men in religious life (the Orders of Friars Minor); the second, in association with St. Clare, organized women in a cloistered contemplative life. When contemporaries of Francis and Clare wished to imitate the life-style, but family or work obligations prevented it, a third group was established. In time it served as a model for other religious communities.

Today nearly a dozen third orders reflect the spirit of the particular religious community with which they are affiliated. For example, Secular Franciscans (largest of the third orders) have a commitment to helping the poor; the Discalced Carmelites give contemplative prayer a high priority; and Oblates of St. Benedict share in monastic life by praying the Liturgy of the Hours in their own daily life and by viewing even the most mundane tasks as a way of glorifying God.

Third order groups are often based in parishes. Members meet regularly for mutual support and prayer, with a priest acting as spiritual adviser. Diocesan priests are eligible to join a third order. A small medal or cloth scapular is worn as a sign of religious vocation in the world. A scapular consists of two pieces of cloth a few inches in diameter, each piece bearing a sacred image. The two are joined by strings and hung about the neck, front and back. The idea originated when devout laypersons in the Middle Ages sought to copy monks and so began wearing a small replica of the work apron monastics wore over their shoulders.

A training period for spiritual formation takes place over a year or longer, depending upon an order's requirements, before the candidate makes a profession. Although no public vows are taken, individuals are free to make private vows. To guide its members in daily life, each order has its own Rule and constitution, approved by the Vatican. Rules differ from one order to another, although each puts emphasis on daily prayer, frequent attendance at Mass and helping others. The overall aim is to grow in love of God, neighbor and self.

Lay Ministry in the Church

Increasingly, people outside of religious life and the ordained clergy are assuming positions in the administration and staffing of chancery offices, once the preserve of priests and religious. In the past, women especially were excluded from career ministry unless they first entered a religious order, but this is no longer the case.

Volunteers are also playing a greater role at the diocesan level as members of commissions or boards in an advisory capacity. They serve as eucharistic ministers in local hospitals under the direction of assigned chaplains, work in special Church ministries or programs to aid the poor, care for the aged, teach English to refugees and give support to families of AIDS victims. And countless Catholics are active volunteers in their own parish-based programs. We will look at parish life in the next chapter.

The Lay Apostolate

Lay apostolates are founded by and for the laity themselves rather than being instituted by the official Church. One of the largest lay apostolates in the world is the Legion of Mary, with more than a million members. It was founded in 1921 in Dublin, Ireland, and transported to the United States in 1931. Legion members commit themselves to prayer and good works of all kinds for the local community and Church. Though they might work under the supervision of a priest, the Legion remains essentially lay-directed.

Probably the best-known American lay apostolate is the
Catholic Worker Movement, founded by Dorothy Day and
Peter Maurin in 1933. It operates Houses of Hospitality for the
poor and marginalized in dozens of cities across the country,
runs soup kitchens and gets involved in peace and justice
issues.

For Further Reading

Chittister, Joan, O.S.B. *Wisdom Distilled from the Daily:
Living the Rule of St. Benedict Today.* San Francisco:
Harper, 1990.

Knight, David M. *Cloud by Day, Fire by Night: The Religious
Life as Passionate Response to God.* Denville, N.J.:
Dimension Books, 1985.

Home of the Church: The Parish

For most Catholics, their parish is "the Church." Parishes come in all sizes and styles: urban, suburban, small town or rural. When a faith community is too small to merit a resident pastor, it may be considered a "mission" attached to a parish, with regularly scheduled—though not necessarily weekly— Mass and administration of sacraments.

The traditional parish with defined geographical boundaries (the "territorial" parish) is the Catholic Church at the neighborhood level. Not so long ago, Catholics were required to register in and attend the parish church within whose boundaries they resided. Though most people continue this practice, dioceses now permit people to join another parish. Those who choose to do so may be seeking a community committed to particular charitable works or a liturgy that meets their spiritual needs or simply a more welcoming congregation. Parish registration is generally required for sacraments such as marriage and Baptism.

Parish Leadership

Traditionally a parish has been headed by a priest-pastor serving full time as both spiritual leader and administrator. In times past, the pastor might also have had two or more younger priests to assist him. Young clerics needed to learn about the day-to-day operations of a parish before being assigned as pastors. An assistant pastor or associate pastor might be likened to an apprentice in a trade.

A diocesan priest entrusted with the pastoral care of a parish is directly responsible to his bishop. If the pastor belongs to a religious order, the arrangement is based on a written agreement between the bishop and the superior of the order. In either case, canon law and local diocesan regulations govern the operations of the parish.

Due to the growing shortage of priests, not only are assistant pastors becoming a thing of the past, but often there are not enough pastors to go around. Rather than close parishes for lack of staff, however, new ways of staffing are being explored and implemented.

One solution has been to assign a parochial minister as pastoral and administrative leader for the parish. Parochial ministers have previous experience in ministry and have studied theology and pastoral ministry at a seminary or another theological institute. They also have strong leadership skills.

In the pastoring role, a parochial minister is qualified to preach, give counseling, take charge of sacramental preparation programs, plan liturgical events, visit the sick, be responsible for the parish budget, oversee maintenance of plant facilities, supervise staff, and even conduct Communion services in the absence of a priest. More than two-thirds of parochial ministers are women, and the majority of these are sisters. Permanent deacons represent a little more than twenty percent of ministers. The rest are primarily laywomen.

Other ways of dealing with a lack of clergy include putting one priest in charge of two parishes, or using the presbyteral team approach in which several priests work together to administer a cluster of parishes. One will then be delegated to direct the team. In rural areas, several congregations may be served by visitations from both a parochial minister and a priest in sacramental ministry.

A parochial minister is supervised by a priest-moderator who is not in residence at the parish, but available if problems should arise. Another priest is designated for liturgical ministry (Mass and the sacraments). Like the moderator, he probably has other responsibilities in the diocese, for example, in a diocesan office.

The priest-pastor or parochial minister often has a pastoral associate, who ministers in a multitude of areas, filling in where needed. This role is frequently filled by a religious sister, though a qualified layperson can fill this role too.

There may also be one or more pastoral assistants on the staff, serving in specific ministerial roles, such as director of religious education, youth minister, liturgist or music minister. The number of assistants depends on the size and vitality of a parish as well as its budget. The positions can be full-time or part-time.

The parish secretary frequently acts as a sounding board for the entire parish and is usually responsible for editing the Sunday bulletin, the weekly newsletter distributed to parishioners after Mass.

As the Catholic population continues to grow, so too do parish programs. Parishes today have many and varied ministries both for their own members and to serve the needs of the broader community. A "mission statement" often identifies parish goals and ways to achieve them.

Parish Life

Parishioners typically share in the leadership of the parish and make their voices heard through representatives they elect to serve on the parish council. The parish council cooperates with the pastor in making decisions for the parish. Members can have input on issues as diverse as whether to pave the church parking lot, continue bingo as a fund-raiser, remove the old communion rail or adopt a sacrificial giving program. A council's effectiveness depends on the enterprise of individuals involved and the pastor's disposition toward shared responsibility.

Canon law requires parishes to have a finance commission either as part of the parish council or as a special group. The members of this commission are parishioners with financial and business expertise. Together with the pastor, they develop and monitor the annual budget, do long-range financial planning, determine costs of new programs and make recommendations to staff and council.

Today a system of Sunday envelopes ensures orderly financial contributions to the parish. This system began in the 1920's, as an alternative to collecting an annual fee (pew rents) from members of the congregation. Other fund-raising projects—dinner-dances, auctions, bazaars and festivals—supplement this regular income. Bingo is a lucrative mainstay in many Catholic parishes, although in recent years it has been criticized on several fronts.

Many dioceses and parishes are moving toward long-range financial development projects and pledge drives that ask people to commit to a level of giving through the year. Stewardship is a concept that returns to the gospel idea of caring for the resources one has been given and using them for the good of all.

Volunteers share in the work of parish ministry and provide the animating force of any parish. According to studies of parish life, volunteers generally care the most about their parish—more so even than pastor and staff. Staff comes and goes; parishioners are apt to remain much longer, some for a lifetime.

Volunteers work in almost every facet of a parish: from flower arranging and vacuuming the sanctuary carpet to serving on the finance commission or collaborating with staff in spiritual renewal programs. Councils, committees, commissions and various organizations contribute to keeping both the faith community and its church building in operating condition.

The primary purpose of any parish is congregational worship, and lay ministers play key roles in liturgical celebrations as eucharistic ministers, readers, altar servers, choir members and ushers. Some parishes schedule an annual commissioning ceremony for lay ministers. A parish may also have a liturgy committee that plans the weekly liturgies and special parish liturgical events.

Other parish organizations involve members in a wide variety of activities. A mainstay in many parishes is the St. Vincent de Paul Society through which men and women give financial and other assistance to the poor. In addition, a parish may develop other forms of outreach to those in need:

operating a poverty center, supporting resettlement of refugees, putting on free Sunday dinners for the homeless. Ministries for the bereaved or homebound and social action groups dealing with peace and justice issues are also ways of responding to community needs.

Popular international and national organizations with parish ties include the Legion of Mary and the Catholic Youth Organization, which provides social, spiritual and recreational activities for youth.

A parish may also have an altar society or altar guild in which women provide support in assorted ways, from laundering altar linens to sponsoring bake sales and maintaining a parish library. Because so many women work outside the home now and have limited free time, volunteer slots are often filled by retired seniors. They can easily be the most active group in a parish, providing a social calendar for themselves and an invaluable service to the parish.

To advance the spiritual life of the parish, Bible study and prayer groups might be organized, or a renewal program instituted to revitalize the congregation. In the past, the parish "mission" served as a sort of retreat, in which a priest trained for this ministry would be brought in to spend a week preaching at evening gatherings and weekend liturgies. Though the message often had a "hellfire-and-brimstone" flavor, churches would be filled. Today high marks are given to renewal programs that focus on small groups coming together to share their faith.

Every parish places a high priority on religious education, perhaps for the adults but always for the youngsters. Much time and energy is devoted to Sunday school classes, with volunteer teachers recruited particularly from among the parents.

The Parochial School

The parochial school system is a unique feature of the American Catholic experience. It started small, with one elementary school for girls opened in 1809 by a young widow, Elizabeth Ann Seton. The religious order she also founded, the

Sisters of Charity, became her source of teachers.

Throughout the nineteenth century, schools multiplied. In 1884 a council of bishops meeting in Baltimore mandated that every parish in the United States establish its own school, although this never happened. In the 1920's, the Confraternity of Christian Doctrine (CCD) program came into being to provide religious education for students attending public schools.

Through the self-sacrifice of teaching orders of sisters and brothers, the number of schools grew to the thousands. At present, across the country, more than 7,000 parochial schools educate close to two million students at the elementary level. The Church also operates high schools, colleges and universities.

Parishes retain control of the schools they establish. A school board or commission may determine tuition costs and set policy. Because tuition never covers the total budget, some parishes underwrite the extra expenses while others give a percentage of parish income for school maintenance, and the school makes up the difference through fund-raisers. Inner-city schools might receive subsidized funding through the diocesan department of education.

Working together to keep schools open gives parishes a sense of mission. Academic standards in parochial schools are generally very high, and many believe that students develop a strong feeling of belonging to their faith community that carries over to adult life.

The American Parish: Yesterday, Today and Tomorrow

Parishes confronting priest shortages can find reassurance in the history of the American Catholic Church. People have always responded to challenges through creative and practical solutions. In the nineteenth century, for example, faced with a shortage of clergy, especially on the frontier, parents baptized their own infants, couples exchanged marriage vows with other than ordained witnesses, burials were conducted in a ritual outside of Mass. "Church" took place at home, reminiscent perhaps of the house Church in primitive Christianity. People coped and faith communities held together between visits from the circuit-riding priest who celebrated Mass and heard confessions.

Worshiping together is the essence of Catholic identity, and Church leaders today have issued guidelines for "priestless Sundays." I recall the first instance of this in my own parish. When our half-time priest-pastor was called away on a Sunday, the sister acting as pastoral associate arranged a Communion service for the congregation according to the guidelines. Neither we nor she knew quite what to expect or what our reaction might be.

The service proceeded with a growing feeling of confidence on both sides. We had an unusual attentiveness to what was happening each step of the way. Our sense that we were all in this together is what being a parish family really means.

For Further Reading

Bausch, William J. *The Hands-On Parish: Reflections and Sessions for Fostering Community.* Mystic, Conn.: Twenty-Third Publications, 1989.

Castelli, Jim, and Joseph Gremillion. *The Emerging Parish: The Notre Dame Study of Catholic Life Since Vatican II.* San Francisco: Harper & Row, 1987.

A Few Good General References

Foy, Felician A., O.F.M., and Rose M. Avato. *Catholic Almanac*. Huntington, Ind.: Our Sunday Visitor, published annually.

Liturgy Training Publications. *Sourcebook for Sundays and Seasons: An Almanac of Parish Liturgy*. Chicago: Liturgy Training Publications, published annually.

Weiser, Francis X. *Handbook of Christian Feasts and Customs: The Year of the Lord in Liturgy and Folklore*. A classic now out of print, but available in many libraries. (Various editions published in the 1950's and 1960's.)